New Church
IN THE CITY

The Work of the Chicago Fellowship of Friends

MARLENE MORRISON PEDIGO

Friends United Press
Richmond, Indiana

LIBRARY OF CONGRESS
Library of Congress Cataloging in Publication Data

Pedigo, Marlene Morrison, 1952-
    New church in the city : the work of the Chicago Fellowship of
Friends / by Marlene Morrison Pedigo.
        p.   cm.
    ISBN 0-944350-05-4
    1. Chicago Fellowship of Friends. 2. Society of Friends—Illinois
— Chicago. 3. City missions—Illinois—Chicago. 4. Chicago (Ill.) —
Church history—20th century.   I. Title.
BX7649. C53P43 1988
289.6'77311 — dc19   88-3867
                                                                     CIP

Cover: Cabrini Homes and Cabrini Extension housing in Chicago.

Scripture quotations are from *The Holy Bible, New International
Version*. Copyright 1973, 1978, 1984 by the International Bible
Society. Used by permission of Zondervan Bible Publishers.

The publisher shares a commitment with the writer for inclusive
language. We chose not to edit historical quotes for this puurpose.

Those who sow in tears
will reap with songs of joy.
He who goes out weeping,
carrying seed to sow,
will return with songs of joy
carrying sheaves with him.

Psalm 126:5,6

Contents

Foreword

Following World War II, the middle-class whites fled the cities of America and moved to the suburbs. The poor who took their places were the blacks from the rural south and a host of people from oppressed third-world countries. The new urbanites have been caught up in a culture of poverty that has often rendered them incapable of handling their everyday tasks. Single-parent homes have become normative, and most of the children born in these cities are born out of wedlock. The rates of juvenile delinquency have soared, and the educational institutions which for previous generations have been instruments for upward mobility have lost their effectiveness.

Into such citadels of despair have ventured small groups of bold Christians, equipped with little more than spiritually-generated compassion and a belief that those who are trapped in urban settings could live out a dream for a better life. As they walked among the poor and the downtrodden, they discovered more than they had expected. In the eyes of the poor and the oppressed, they were able to see the Jesus whom they loved, and that changed everything.

If people serve the poor out of a sense of noble obligation, they end up on ego trips; but, if, when serving the poor, one senses the presence of Christ in the downtrodden, perceptions are changed and attitudes are transformed. Those who see Jesus in the hurting of the world recognize that it is a privilege to serve them and that the minister can only ask the question, "Are we worthy?"

The Chicago Fellowship of Friends represents the best of those who have made the poor of the city the focus of mission. Working through a variety of vehicles that include Bible studies, camping experiences, recreational programs and cultural enrichment programs, these servants of God, whom we like to call the Quakers, have made a difference. Focusing on Cabrini-Green, an area of three blocks by five, that houses 8,000 people, they have served the kingdom well. This book will give you some idea as to what they have accomplished, but only eternity will measure the worth of their efforts.

I have been amazed at the low level of expenditure employed by this group of Quakers. They seem to be doing incredible things with very little money. They move by inspiration and by wisdom that comes from none other than the Holy Spirit. George Fox, the founder of the Society of Friends, would be proud of these heirs to his movement; but, more important, one can hear a voice echoing down the corridors of time, and it is the voice of Jesus saying, "Well done, thou good and faithful servants."

I have visited the work of The Chicago Fellowship of Friends, and I can assure you this book understates the magnificence that is being accomplished. Read it carefully. Be inspired. Be challenged to go and do likewise, for the cities of America wait for the message of the kingdom.

Tony Campolo
Professor of Sociology
Eastern College

Violent Legacy

1

*"No pain, no palm, no thorns, no throne, no gall,
no glory, no cross, no crown."*

William Penn

My heart was pounding and I wondered if I would leave
alive. What had started as a basketball scrimmage between two
community teams in a youth center on Chicago's West Side
had turned into a small riot. My husband, Steve, was coach for
our team. As we walked into the new spacious gymnasium
lined with bleachers, the center's director remarked that they
rarely had outside teams play in their facilities. Why wouldn't
anyone love to play here?

As the ball game started, neighborhood youth began filling
the bleachers to cheer for their team. Although our team played
hard, they were losing. In the closing minutes of the game, one
of our guards made a senseless remark to an opposing player,
and a fistfight erupted on the floor. Rather than trying to stop
it, the other team members began swinging, too. The basketball
game immediately became a free-for-all. No longer spectators,
the young people in the stands spilled onto the floor to join the

brawl.

On one side four or five young men began swinging at one of our forwards. As Steve attempted to separate them, he got a swift hard left to the jaw. Our tall, muscular center struggled to keep the heads of two contenders under each arm in a head lock and out of further violence. In the meantime, the guard who had started the whole incident quietly slipped to the corner of the gymnasium.

I rose to my feet in the bleachers, but I was too stunned and frightened to move. I could hear whistles blowing as adults shoved contenders out of the building.

The center's director ran down the hall to telephone the police. Our team waited, locked in the gym for protection. The mob outside pounded on the door and screamed threats of further violence. When the police finally escorted us to our van, we realized the mob had done more than threaten. In the darkness we picked our way through broken glass to find that the mob had smashed the lights, torn off the windshield wipers and flattened all the tires.

We had just moved to the Chicago area. Unknowingly we had crossed one of the invisible "turf" boundaries which are a harsh reality of Chicago's street gangs. We had learned the hard way.

I struggled to force back the tears as we drove down the freeway towards home. My first impulse was to tell Steve that I was going back to my parents' farm in Iowa. At home that night, Steve and I poured out our fears and prayed for future guidance. Through the silence of our prayers we received an inner confirmation that this was where we were supposed to be. Although we had suffered in the process of ministry, our main calling was to focus upon obediently following Christ Jesus. We were only experiencing the urban ethos which was a part of the young peoples' lives. But there was more violence to come.

"Fred has been shot!"

I was sitting in our living room watching TV after our

Wednesday evening youth program when Steve burst into the room with his shocking news.

"I had pulled up the van along the Chicago Avenue basketball courts to drop off the high school kids from our meeting when suddenly Carolyn came running to the van in panic asking me to take Fred and her to the hospital. A sniper had just shot him as they were walking down Larrabee Street. In the meantime a paramedic drove by, and we flagged him down. As they treated Fred's shoulder wound, Carolyn called their parents from the pay phone on the street. Then I drove her over to Henrotin Hospital," Steve said.

Steve turned off the TV and sat down on the couch next to me. As he took my hand in his I knew it was time for prayer.

"Lord, we come to you with heavy hearts tonight. We are asking for a special blessing for Fred. May your healing power be upon him that his wound will not be serious and he will not suffer in great pain. May your peace be with Fred, Carolyn, and their families," Steve pled.

"Dear Jesus, I just want to pray for an end to the violence in the community. May you shield other teens in the community from danger. Protect us from evil and bring us your peace," I prayed.

We knew Fred well, and he was not a gang member. He had done nothing to provoke the shooting that night. Fred was not the only one who had suffered, either; other incidents of shooting already had occurred that year. The attention of many people became focused upon Cabrini-Green, the Chicago neighborhood in which we had chosen to locate our youth ministry. Slowly I came to realize that, as is often the case, there was a long economic and political history behind the community's violence.

As Chicago grew, the Near North Side became the home of poor immigrants coming to the city for employment. Located near the Chicago River factories and the downtown area, this community was within easy access of work opportunities. Numerous immigrant groups settled in the area and later moved as they acquired finances to afford better housing in other areas of the city or in the suburbs. The housing continued to deteriorate. It was in this area that Dwight Moody centered his ministry in the late nineteenth century.

By the early 1900s the Near North Side was known as "Little Hell." During the era of Prohibition it was the setting for gang-style fights and organized crime which controlled the alcohol business. The Historical Museum of Chicago contains a map of the various gangs in existence at this time. Not only was this area the scene of gang warfare, part of it was labeled "death corner" because fifty homicides already had occurred in a small area on Oak Street. Even at that time the area had a reputation for being poor and violent!

During the early 1940s the City of Chicago was faced with a severe housing problem. In an attempt to provide a solution to the dirt-floor flats which were located on the Near North Side, the city designed plans for one of their first public housing ventures which became known as the Cabrini Homes. Named after an Italian-American saint, Mother Cabrini, this new housing was hoped to be the answer to the community's problems. The old tenant flats were replaced by new terrace townhouses between Oak Street and Chicago Avenue.

This new housing venture was soon followed by two more phases, the Cabrini Extension and the William Green Homes. In an effort to provide housing for more individuals in a limited amount of space, this new housing included high rise buildings which ranged in size from seven to nineteen floors. The combined housing units became known as Cabrini-Green.

Another change occurred on the Near North Side during this time. After the construction of the original Cabrini homes, the population on the Near North Side began another transition. The black population from the South, which had been attracted to Chicago for employment during World War II, now moved into the Near North Side and replaced the Italian community.

Since this was now public housing, the government became the landlord and controlled the demographics of the population who lived in the area. Their housing regulations created a community with a focus upon poor, single-parent families. Federal guidelines also mandated a community in perpetual transition, since residents who began working would automatically be required to pay 30 percent of their gross income. Since most residents would rather rent a better-quality apartment or buy their own home instead of paying $400 to $500 a month for rent, many positive role models were often forced from the community because of financial pressures once they received a job.

By the 1960s the population of Cabrini-Green had swelled to approximately 26,000 in a three-by-six block area. When the 1968 riots occurred across the country, National Guard tanks roamed the streets of the neighborhood. Cabrini-Green once again became known for its violence when two policemen were killed. The earlier problems of gang violence and illegal substance trade by organized crime surfaced again. Rather than alcohol, the problem was now a wide variety of narcotics. The new population of women and children who now lived in the area faced the extreme difficulty of protecting themselves from these evils.

Today the community has become divided across boundaries similar to those which existed during Prohibition. The northeastern section is known as the turf for the Cobra Stones (El Rukns) and the Vicelords. The southwestern section is known as the turf for the Black Gangster Disciples. Young people are recruited early by the gangs, often when they are only eight or ten years of age and want to belong to a peer group. Rather than joining Boy Scouts or Campfire Girls, they become identified with a gang — a group which dictates their lifestyle and future. The El Rukns' symbol is the crescent moon and five-point star. Their members are told not to eat pork and to always wear a hat. The Black Gangster Disciples' symbol is the six-point star and the Satanic pitchfork. Each gang's turf boundaries are openly marked with these symbols on the corners of the buildings; their members openly identify themselves by the direction their hats are tilted, a variety of hand gestures and the colors of their clothes.

The gangs become an alternative family and authority for the children who are involved. Young people are tutored in a life of crime by the older gang members. Children are used to hold the weapons or sell drugs, since the sentence for a child is much lighter in Juvenile Court than in Adult Court. Their reward is a sense of belonging to a peer group, easy access to drugs, and access to the girl members of the gang. Members are given rank according to their loyalty and performance in the gang. A foot soldier is one of the lowest ranks and is given minor jobs, such as guarding the entrance to his building all hours of the day.

Unlike a typical youth clique, a gang is easy to join, but very difficult to leave. To get out of a gang, members may have to go through the "line." There fellow gang members gather in parallel lines armed with chains, bats or other weapons. The members who want to exit the gang must run through the line successfully to leave. If they fall to the ground in the process of running through the line, they will not be able to leave. Even jail is not an exit. The same gangs control these institutions and further tutor members for a lifetime of crime. In other efforts to leave a gang, many families have sent their children out of the community to stay with relatives.

The residents of Cabrini are frustrated by the chronic problems. They want much more for their children, yet they feel powerless to change the forces which affect their lives. They are a community of primarily children and women. Of the 8,755 residents, 5,787 are youth. Approximately 93 percent of the families are single parent.[1] They have many questions, but they receive few solutions.

Often the institutions which are designed to provide the answers fall short of the goals. The Chicago school system laments the statistics which indicate that children graduate from high school with grammar-school reading scores. The high schools report high dropout rates. School properties are regularly guarded by police officers to control violence. With such a large centralized school system, it is difficult for individuals from the community to make a lasting impact upon their schools.

The landlord for Cabrini-Green, the Chicago Housing Authority, also struggles to be effective. Often residents wait weeks for repairs to be completed on their apartments. Due to a lack of funds to make the needed roof repairs in many buildings, residents are moved from their apartments. Cabrini residents also live with the fear that their homes will be sold by the C.H.A. to a real estate developer since the land is near Lake Michigan and Chicago's central business district. The central offices of the C.H.A. struggle to acquire funds from the shrinking federal housing budget, while the federal government boldly spends more than half of its budget on the military.

Security for the residents is difficult. The police department strives to provide law and order, yet gangs and drugs fill the community. No one seems to have the answers for why residents must live in fear of violence and retaliation. In search of justice, many individuals take matters into their own hands out of frustration.

Some people advocate the destruction of Cabrini-Green. They insist that the buildings are the source of the problem; people should be moved away. Yet they fail to understand the core issues of the community were present decades before the buildings were built. If the buildings were destroyed, how would these core issues be addressed? What would happen to the people? What would happen to the sense of community which does exist among some of the residents? Why should all the good people be punished for what a minority in the community are doing? For many, Cabrini-Green is where their friends and family live — their sisters, their cousins, their grandparents.

During the recent decades, many churches fled to the suburbs as immigrant groups from across the world settled in the cities. Rather than staying to learn new ways of ministry, these churches abandoned their properties for new facilities which would better serve "their people." Some denominations even destroyed their church buildings after the congregation moved. Some rationalized that it was solely the government's responsibility to be concerned with the poor; "isn't that why we pay taxes?" However, although the government can provide money, it cannot address the spiritual problems within the individual and community. This is where the church's message is needed. Do we care?

Growing into Urban Ministry

2

*"And so let this serve to stop that opposing Spirit
that would limit the Power and Spirit of the Lord
Jesus, whose Spirit is poured upon all flesh, both
Sons and Daughters, now in his Resurrection...."*
Margaret Fell

I grew up in rural Grinnell, Iowa, the "bread basket" of our
country, where I knew very few outward needs. The realities of
war, poverty, illiteracy and crime were virtually unknown in
my daily existence. My family had been farmers for generations in the same township from the time my ancestors first
purchased the deep, rich virgin soil from the State of Iowa.

Often in the cool of the evening as the distant stars began to
appear, I would walk across the fields of my parents' farm
toward my favorite "reflection spot." The fragrance of freshly
mown hay, the nightly locust chorus, and the soft rustle of the
corn leaves moving in the summer breeze easily erased the
activities of the day from my mind. I would lie down in the
pasture and turn my eyes to the stars. I wondered at the
greatness of God and His creation. In the peace which sur-

9

rounded me, I prayed for answers to my inner unrest and to know the purpose for which God had designed my life.

As a child, I had heard stories of my great-grandfather, J. T. Molloy, who, as a convinced Quaker, had traveled widely in the ministry. My favorite story was about his death. He thrilled at the feeling of going over the top of a hill in the newly invented automobile, and he often told others he wished he could go to the top of a hill and just keep going upward. One day J. T. was driving down a country road to deliver a hog loaded in the back of his truck when he suffered a fatal heart attack. Later, he was found in his truck on the side of the road at the top of a hill. I decided that he got his wish.

My grandparents also influenced me. Each day after my grandmother had washed the morning dishes, she read a Scripture passage and a devotional message before she entered a time of prayer. I can still see my grandmother in her rocking chair with her well-worn black Bible open on her lap as she read to us. In later life, she regained her speech after a severe stroke by faithfully repeating the Twenty-Third Psalm which she had committed to memory. She was certainly a "living saint" in my life.

Finally, my spiritual life was further nurtured by my own family. I am the first of seven children in a tightly knit farm family. My parents instilled the discipline of church attendance and modeled their own commitment to the Lord. While other children were at home watching cartoons on television, we gathered as a family to sing, listen, and participate in Quaker meeting for worship.

It was through my own family's small Quaker meeting that I discovered the reality of Christ Jesus and the inner peace for which I yearned. Its caring community created a lasting impression in my life. Mrs. Greene, a woman in her nineties, led vocal prayer during worship every week even when she was physically suffering. Another member, Andy, loved to select choruses to sing during evening meetings for worship. Betty, my Sunday School teacher, invited us over to her home to eat homemade ice cream. These people created a sense of belonging within me and modeled what the Christian faith meant.

While I was in high school, a Quaker evangelistic team from Ireland, John and Dorothy Sinton, visited us for one week of nightly meetings. One evening, Dorothy Sinton delivered one of the most memorable sermons of my life. A recorded Friends minister, Dorothy was of average build in her late middle age. When she rose to speak, she did not raise her voice nor pound on the pulpit. Instead, she opened her Bible to read Isaiah 29:13-16:

> The Lord says:
> "These people come near to me
>   with their mouth
> and honor me with their lips,
>   but their hearts are far from me.
> Their worship of me
>   is made up only of rules taught by
>   men.
> Therefore once more I will astound
>   these people
> with wonder upon wonder;
> the wisdom of the wise will perish,
>   the intelligence of the intelligent
>   will vanish."
>
> Woe to those who go to great depths
>   to hide their plans from the Lord,
> who do their work in darkness and
>   think,
>   "Who sees us? Who will
>   know?"
> You turn things upside down,
>   as if the potter were thought to be
>   like the clay!
> Shall what is formed say to him who
>   formed it,
>   "He did not make me"?
> Can the pot say of the potter,
>   "He knows nothing"?

Each of our lives *is* like a lump of clay with tremendous potential. We can place ourselves in the hands of our Creator, as master potter, who will fashion us with great care into a vessel which can be used for his service. That night I openly committed myself to becoming whatever God would want me to be and to serve the Lord to the best of my ability.

Another formative experience occurred during the summer of my junior year of college. One evening at the close of an evangelism conference, thousands of college students gathered to fill the Cotton Bowl to hear Billy Graham. The challenge before us as we left the conference was to take what we had learned "on the mountain" into the world daily. We must not abandon the church, we were told, but seek to strengthen it and spread its message. As we each held a candle and passed the light of its glow across the Cotton Bowl, we sang, "Pass It on." That moment I deepened my commitment to follow Jesus Christ even into the toughest "world" situation.

I did not realize at this time where this decision for commitment would lead me. However, through the man I would marry, God opened an unexpected door for urban ministry.

During my freshman year at William Penn College, I had come to know Steve Pedigo, an energetic classmate from Milwaukee. We dated steadily in our sophomore year. One spring night in May, he broke off our relationship by merely saying that he was not ready to become serious. I was crushed! With the breakup I realized how much I had come to love him—his wit, his love for life, and his commitment to his faith. I tried in vain to get him to reconsider his decision. With pain I watched him date others that next year, and I tried to put our relationship behind me. Yet, through those next few months my own faith grew steadily, and I could sense God using me in new avenues of ministry.

One spring night almost one year later I was sitting at my desk alone in my dormitory room reading Scripture. As I read a passage on prayer, I sensed the Holy Spirit speaking to me to pray for Steve. I had prayed about this relationship many times in the past, but at that moment there was an urgency to the promptings. As I arose I felt a lightness of heart and an air of expectation that God was moving in Steve's life in some way unknown to me.

That night after dinner, I drove with a group of college friends to a revival at a small Friends meeting in a nearby town. The minister's sermon that night clearly challenged us all to deepen our commitment to Jesus Christ. It was a joy for me to see one of my friends walk forward for prayer to become a Christian. I eagerly rose to join her in prayer support.

As I walked back down the aisle, Steve walked up to me. "I need to talk with you," he said. Imagining it was in reference to the evening's events, I casually remarked, "Sure, what is it?"

Slowly and with great sincerity in the midst of the meeting-house filled with people, he looked deep into my eyes and said, "I believe God is calling us back together."

I was in shock! After one year of tearful pain I had finally surrendered the whole relationship to God. Now God was giving me the "desires of my heart." As we hugged each other, I knew at that moment our relationship had been called together by the Lord. In the middle of the meetinghouse, Steve proposed to me, and God revealed to me greater insight into my future purpose and ministry.

Following our college graduation and our wedding, we spent our first summer together on the staff of a large camp in Southern Wisconsin. Each week there, a new group of two to four hundred children from Chicago had the opportunity to have a brief vacation and hear us share about our faith. It was frustrating to realize they often would return to extremely difficult environments to try to live out what they had heard.

Since Steve came from Milwaukee, he easily identified with them. His father was a traveling salesman and was often away from home. Frustrated and lonely, his mother suffered with alcoholism in later life. To avoid the pain and conflict at home, Steve often found himself on the streets with his friends. Other times he would walk the lakefront alone in the evening and

14

wish someone would reach out to him. After Steve became a Christian and realized how much God loved him, he dreamed of finding a ministry where he could communicate the Good News of Christ to other urban young people. Ideally he wanted to be with teens before and after their camping experience to help them understand the full dynamics of the Christian life.

As Steve prayed for guidance, an opportunity for ministry arose. During the middle of his training at Asbury Theological Seminary, a fellow summer-camp staff member invited us to Chicago to help begin a youth ministry in Cabrini-Green, a government housing development on the Near North Side of the city. Quickly the doors opened for Steve to transfer to North Park Theological Seminary, obtain our housing, and begin the new youth ministry.

As Steve excitedly made the arrangements, I was hesitant. I wondered if I was ready for such a major change. I was afraid of the unknown. As I resigned my positions, I sought counsel from my employer at the day care center where I worked.

Irma Morris, a recorded Friends minister also from Iowa, had unconsciously been serving as my role model during the time I had worked for her. Through Irma's dedication, a babysitting service in her home had grown into a day care center for over one hundred children in the basement of a church. Her love for the Lord and the families she served was evident to all who worked with her.

On the day I resigned in 1976, I walked into her office and slipped into a chair near her desk. Without hesitation, I poured out my anxieties about moving to Chicago. I was a country girl. Would I be able to adjust to this radically different setting? I enjoyed the cocoon-like environment of seminary life and the nurturing I received from a setting where I was surrounded primarily by Christians. Could God so soon be calling me to spread my wings and leave behind my secure environment?

Irma patiently listened to my heart's turmoil and reassured me with a simple statement reflective of her own genuine, deep faith. "God never calls people without also equipping them for the ministry. You must trust Him to do this as you step out in faith."

Her words were etched in my memory for years to come. Her confident witness that day gave me the strength to leave behind my security in order to be faithful.

Just a few days later I was helping Steve pack our few belongings in our old black Plymouth station wagon. We hitched up a rented U-Haul trailer and drove down the interstate to our new home in Chicago, confident that God was leading us.

After our arrival in Chicago, my involvement seemed merely to be centered upon going to the basketball games Steve coached because I didn't want to sit home alone. This ministry was his dream. I was along as a spectator. Yet was I being called to make a commitment to ministry, too? Could the Lord use me effectively in such a different culture from my background? I prayed that God would show me if I should become more active in the ministry.

One night as I walked into the gymnasium to join Steve and the team, I noticed the two teenage girls who had come along with the team sitting by themselves. I walked over and sat down next to them. As we waited for the game to start, I introduced myself and discovered they were the girlfriends of two of the team members. During the game we cheered our team on together and shared the joy of their victory. Afterwards I invited the girls and some of the team members over to our house for hot dogs and a game of Pit. By the end of the evening I had my answer from the Lord. Besides being a support for Steve and his ministry, I could have a definite ministry to these girls.

It took several months of meeting young people at basketball games, on the playground and through invitations to our home, before we could plan our first formal meeting. Our site for the gathering was in the living room of a home. As the teens arrived, we invited them to have a seat on the floor. To our surprise, there soon was barely enough space to walk through the roomful of fifty young people! Our core group of teens from the basketball games had invited their friends, and a buzz of excitement hung in the air.

As the night progressed, I realized we were having a significant impact on the lives of several teens. On one side of the room sat Carol. She was one of the teenage girls I had developed a relationship with at the weekly basketball games. Now her face beamed as she sang, "He—'s Alive," and clapped to the rhythmical tune. One of Steve's basketball players, Ken, readily rose to his feet to join in a skit. His leadership helped to relax his peers as they laughed in response to the antics. We ended the evening with a brief devotional, and the faces of the teens reflected their eagerness to participate in the group. Months of cultivating our ministry through listening and caring had created a solid foundation for the program. Throughout the following school year we continued to hold weekly youth meetings, in addition to organizing another basketball team.

As the summer approached, we again prepared to take the teens to summer camp. I was excited to have girls in the group to whom I had ministered over the year. The activities at camp were designed to help them put behind the pressures at home, build their self-image through new experiences, and expose them to a bigger picture of God's world. We climbed mountains, rode horses, went swimming, played volleyball, had barbecues, and held nightly meetings to explain the basics of the Christian life. Amidst the beauty of the Rocky Mountains, the scent of the stately pine trees, and the moonlight on a clear night, the young people were reminded of their Creator and God's place in their lives.

After a week of long hours with the girls at camp, I rested my head against the bus window and tried to get some sleep as we headed home to Chicago. Since it was late, I began to doze off. Suddenly, one of the teenage girls sat down next to me.

"I'm not ready to go home," she pled. "I wish I could stay at camp. Life is so much easier there."

Slowly she shared with me her past and some of the pain she experienced in her family and in the community. I listened quietly to the ache in her heart.

"You may not be able to change your environment, but I know a way you can change yourself and gain the power to deal with your environment," I replied.

Just then we were joined by her girlfriends who had overheard us talking. They both listened intently as I shared what it meant to become a Christian. With heads bowed and the hum of the bus wheels in the background, we prayed together.

As the months passed, I found more of my time devoted to ministry. While Steve was attending classes at North Park and working as an intern, I worked first as a substitute teacher and then a church secretary. However, almost every spare moment was dedicated to youth ministry. Before I knew it, my ministry to the girls had grown to the point that I quit my other jobs and began working full time in youth ministry along Steve's side. I was suddenly in full time ministry, and I loved it!

In 1977 my home meeting recommended to Iowa Yearly Meeting that both Steve and I be recorded (ordained) as ministers within the Religious Society of Friends. Since Steve was a seminary student, it was a relatively simple procedure. However, our finances did not allow me to attend school with Steve. Thus, I enrolled into an independent study project and came under the guidance of an appointed committee. Now I spent hours studying areas of church history, theology, and practical ministry.

As I read volume after volume and wrote papers on various topics, I sensed the rich heritage of which I was a part. For more than three hundred years Quaker women had been active in the ministry. The lives of these women became personal role models as I read of their witness.

Margaret Fell, for instance, was known as the "Mother of Quakerism." During the English Reformation in the mid 1600s, her dedication and zeal led her to open her home as one of the early centers for traveling Quaker ministers. In addition to serving as a political advocate for Quakers imprisoned for religious convictions, Margaret wrote theological statements defending the Friends peace testimony and the practice of women in the ministry. She eventually married George Fox, the founder of the Religious Society of Friends.

Mary Dyer, another personal favorite, was a Friends minister she was hung on the Boston Common. Her death prompted such a great outcry from her friends and neighbors that shortly thereafter religious freedom was granted by the local magistrates. Her obedience to divine leading opened the way for religious freedom in this country.

The ministry of Elizabeth Fry in the early 1800s served as my personal example of a woman who dared to change a social evil. Concerned about the wretched conditions in England's prisons, she began a ministry to the women and children in Newgate Prison. Through Bible studies, schools for children, employment for the women, and other methods of reorganization and reform, Elizabeth Fry radically altered society's treatment of those in prison.

I began to read the Bible with new awareness. I noted the number of women who not only followed Christ, but also served as prophetesses, deacons, and proclaimers of the Good News. I was especially drawn to the biblical couple, Priscilla and Aquila. They had met Paul while he had stayed in their home during the birth of the Corinthian church. They then journeyed with him to begin the church at Ephesus. When Apollos attempted to mislead the church, Priscilla and Aquila invited him to their home and "explained to him the way of God more adequately" (Acts 18:26). They also later journeyed to Rome where a church met in their home (Romans 16:3-5). This New Testament clergy couple also became my personal role model.

The more I studied, the greater became my zeal for the ministry. Although some tried to deter me by saying it was perhaps enough that Steve was a minister, I would not relinquish my vision. On a warm August evening during the 1979 sessions of the Iowa Yearly Meeting of Friends, the vision became a reality.

It felt like I was coming home as I walked into Spencer Chapel of William Penn College and recognized faces of personal friends, family and fellow Quakers I had come to love. Many memorable moments had occurred in this room for me during college. Tonight would become another one to add to my mind's album. Earlier in the day at a business session a number of individuals spoke in favor of my recording, and it had received approval. Tonight it would be publicly affirmed.

Following an open time of singing, I was called to join the leaders of Iowa Yearly Meeting at the front of the meeting room. Steve stood at my side. My parents were directly behind me. Dressed in a black suit, I held a new black Bible given to me by my parents earlier in the evening. I was filled with joy overflowing, and I beamed with smiles and gazed at the faces in the crowded room before me.

The Superintendent of the yearly meeting rose to the microphone and read to all:

> The word of the Lord came to me, saying,
> "Before I formed you in the womb, I
>   knew you,
> before you were born, I set you
>   apart;
> I appointed you as a prophet to
>   the nations."

> "Ah, Sovereign Lord," I said, "I do not know how to speak; I am only a child."

> But the Lord said to me, "Do not say, 'I am only a child.' You must go to everyone I send you to and say whatever I command you. Do not be afraid of them, for I am with you and will rescue you," declares the Lord.

> Then the Lord reached out his hand and touched my mouth and said to me, "Now, I have put my words in your mouth. See, today I appoint you over nations and kingdoms to uproot and tear down, to destroy and overthrow, to build and to plant."
>
> Jeremiah 1:4-10

Turning to me, the Iowa Yearly Meeting Superintendent affirmed that God had already ordained me in ministry. At this time the yearly meeting was publicly recording this divine ordination. He charged me to remember that I must continue to remain faithful to being God's spokesperson to all to whom I am called, and then he shook my hand.

I beamed with joy as I accepted the certificate of recording and walked off the platform. After the meeting for worship a long line of friends shook my hand, hugged me, and spoke words of encouragement. This public affirmation of my ministry gave me a tremendous sense of support and renewed confidence.

A few months later I found myself having lunch with a friend in a restaurant on the Near North Side of Chicago. As our waitress brought our food to the table, I began to share with her my recent recording as a minister and my satisfaction working with youth ministry.

As I reached to take another bite of my cheeseburger, she challenged me, "You know you really should go to seminary."

"Yes, but seminary is expensive, and I really don't need to have the additional training for my denomination," I argued. "If I went back to school I would have less time to spend in the community working with people."

I listened as she explained her experience in seminary which prepared her later for an active ministry with InterVarsity. I continued to ask questions as we finished our lunch and walked out the door of the restaurant. Since others also had been urging me with the same message, I wondered if God was trying to tell me to take another step of faith.

I shared my leading with Steve and began to pray. Inwardly I made a covenant with God that I would begin seminary if He would open the doors. That year I began at McCormick Theological Seminary with full financial aid. The door was wide open!

The
First Step

3

"There is one, even Christ Jesus, that can speak to thy condition."

George Fox

"Lord, we need your guidance if we are to begin a church."
This had been our prayer when we first dreamed of the
Fellowship of Friends. For nearly five years as Steve finished
seminary we had been involved in youth work in the Cabrini-
Green community. As the teens graduated from high school,
we saw the need to develop a ministry which would continue
the discipleship process. Also, we were concerned with the
necessity to no longer be "Lone Rangers" in the ministry, but
to be a part of a community of faith from Cabrini-Green who
would share in the decision-making process and provide ministry leadership. It became evident that our style of ministry
was influenced by our commitment to our Quaker faith. We
had been urged to begin a church.

While on vacation in 1980, we decided to stop at Friends
United Meeting, the headquarters of one group of Quakers.
Since our appointment was for early morning, we spent the

21

night at their guest lodgings.

Before leaving for our appointment, we knelt beside our bed in prayer to pour out our hearts to the Lord.

"Lord, this is a real step of faith, to ask Quakers to give financial support to people they have never met for a ministry they have never seen," Steve prayed.

"You know I find it hard to step out in faith," I pled in prayer, "so we really need a miracle this morning if you want us to pursue this new direction."

As we waited again in silence, I could feel the warm sunshine flooding the room around us. The peace of God began to fill our hearts. Only a few minutes remained before our appointment with the leaders of Friends United Meeting when we rose confidently from our time of prayer.

Moments later we gathered with three staff members of Friends United Meeting in the office of Kara Cole, the Administrative Secretary. Steve had telephoned her just days before asking for an appointment to share about our ministry. Our presentation that day included photos of the ministry in Cabrini-Green which we had arranged in a dime-store picture album. We enthusiastically shared our vision to begin a Friends meeting out of the youth ministry in which we had been involved.

As we talked, I sensed their concern and interest. My heart nearly burst with happiness when I heard it mentioned that one of the Friends United Meeting's projects no longer needed funding. Their World Ministries program had been wondering what to do with this surplus of finances during the last few weeks. The staff suggested that our dream be proposed to their Board meetings in the fall as a new project for Quakers. What a miraculous answer to prayer!

During the following months of the summer, we busied ourselves with the renovation of a newly acquired two-family brick home on the Near West Side of Chicago which was to become the initial center of our Friends ministry. Located only a few blocks from the high school attended by many of the youth in our ministry, it was also within walking distance of

Cabrini-Green. However, we soon faced conflict within the community.

One warm August evening as Steve and I returned to Chicago after a visit with friends and family in Iowa, we were greeted by our next-door neighbors with a look of alarm in their faces. While we were gone someone had set fire to our garage!

I listened intently to the details they recalled: it had occurred at night while they had been sleeping... they had smelled smoke... someone had piled garbage against the garage door to torch it... the fire department put out the fire and acted as if it was a common occurrence.

That night as I struggled to fall asleep, thoughts of awakening in the middle of flames plagued me. Tears trickled down my cheeks as I fought back my wildest fears. Why would someone want to burn our garage? Steve held me in his arms as we prayed together seeking God's peace and guidance for the future.

In the months which followed, we learned that Chicago's fires were not always set by Mrs. O'Leary and her infamous cow. In a city which prides itself on having strong neighborhoods, the real estate agents do not warn you that it sometimes comes at the price of bigotry. The burning of property of newcomers with the wrong racial background is not uncommon. Others less fortunate than we had not merely lost their garage to fire, but their car, their possessions, and their home.

In the attempt to cross racial barriers we felt like aliens in our own country, a nation known for being a haven for the "...huddled masses yearning to breathe free." The black community wondered what our ulterior motive might be for coming to Cabrini-Green. Our immigrant neighbors worried that we might move Cabrini blacks onto their block.

Shortly after our garage burned for a second time, Steve and a volunteer were showered with dirt and rocks as they walked down the sidewalk to our home. Their assailants were a group of teenagers from the community. Later that day Steve sat on the front steps of our house and waited for the boys to walk past. As he saw two of them approach, Steve said, "Hey, boys why did you throw those rocks?"

Trying to ignore Steve, the boys ran to their house. One of the boys went inside while the other lingered on the steps outside. Steve walked over to him.

"Hey, why did you throw those rocks?" Steve again probed the teen.

" 'Cause you're bringin' blacks into the neighborhood," he said toughly.

"Well, I live here just like you do. I own a house here. Don't throw rocks again," Steve replied.

Suddenly one of the boys' mothers appeared in the doorway.

"Are you going to move blacks into our neighborhood?" she questioned Steve.

"I'm not doing that," he replied.

"Well, I thought you were," she said defensively.

"If you want to know something, why don't you ask me? It is hard to understand what is troubling you when you throw rocks. Next time, ask," Steve encouraged her.

"I will," was her response as she turned back into her home.

Shortly thereafter at the request of her son, Ron, Steve gave the woman a ride to the hospital when she became ill. He also encouraged her son to pursue his G.E.D. Ron began to drop by our home to talk to Steve about what was happening in his life and to receive encouragement. We rejoiced when Ron later gave his life to the Lord! Thus, as we began the ministry of the Fellowship of Friends, we asked that we might be a witness of Christ's universal love to all those around us.

For several years during our youth ministry, we had led Bible studies in our home for teenagers from Cabrini-Green. Usually we met for an hour of reading, discussion and prayer followed by a time of fellowship. Over the years the Bible studies began to include more young adults. Slowly the focus of these groups became one of worship.

When this transition began, we moved the time of the Bible study to Sunday afternoons in the living room of our home. Our setting was informal. Folding chairs created a semi-circle arrangement with a piano in the center.

The first change in the program included the addition of a time of singing on Sunday afternoons. We sang choruses from our weekly youth programs in the beginning. As the weeks passed, we introduced "How Great Thou Art" and other church hymns. Next the young people asked to have a choir. With a little practice they soon sang, "Somebody's knocking on your door..."

Besides adding music to our Bible studies, we also began to lengthen the time of prayer to become periods of open worship as is customary within the Religious Society of Friends. We talked about the priesthood of believers and encouraged everyone to express their inner hearts to God and to the gathered meeting. As heads were bowed in respect, the room was filled with a peaceful silence.

"Thank you, God, for waking me up this morning and giving me life."

"Dear Lord, please look after my mother. She is really going through a struggle right now. Help her to turn to you."

"I need your help God! Guide me and keep me from the temptations around me."

The Spirit of God could be sensed in the earnestness of those who prayed. A final change was the introduction of sermons. Steve and I continued to share the importance of a deeper faith commitment to the young people. We stressed discipleship and evangelism. The young people appreciated this time of teaching from the Scriptures and felt it spoke to their spiritual needs.

Soon we began talking about what it means to be a Quaker. I can still remember some of the first comments.

"I thought Quakers were the people who make oatmeal."

"Didn't Quakers live in the olden days? I thought they all died."

"Aren't Quakers the people who dress in black clothes and wear black hats?"

Their questions reflected how few people today understand the beliefs of the Religious Society of Friends, more commonly known as Quakers. We had to start from the beginning. We passed out booklets to read and spent time discussing Quakerism.

With great care we tried to explain about the English Reformation and the religious turmoil which occurred between 1530 and 1600. First the country's religion was Catholicism, and then the ruler would change and Protestantism would be endorsed. It was very confusing for the lay people since at this time there was a state church and until 1642 everyone was required to be a member and pay tithes. With the printing of books and Bibles in England, people began to meet in small groups to read the Bible for themselves. As they began to question the practices of the established church, new denominations were formed. One of these new groups of gathered believers was the Quakers. They were the left-wing branch of the Puritan movement.

As a young man in England, George Fox had become disillusioned with the hypocrisy which he found in the established church and its rituals. After seeking for truth from religious leaders of his time and reading the Bible for himself, he discovered the answer. One day as he was walking he heard a voice which said to him, "There is one, even Christ Jesus, that can speak to thy condition." Fox realized that each individual could personally encounter the living Christ which was within him or her. By listening to this inner voice, not only would peoples' lives be transformed in obedience, but they would receive guidance for transforming the world around them. From this obedience came Quaker testimonies of honesty, justice, equality, simplicity, peace, and the sacramental lifestyle. Fox told this message unceasingly to those around him.

Members of the Society of Friends were seen as radicals by the established church of that day. They were imprisoned and flogged by the magistrates. Their nickname, "Quakers," came from a judge who said these individuals seemed to quake in the presence of God. However, their faith would not be destroyed. Their evangelistic spirit resulted in a rapid expansion of Quakerism not only throughout England but in the colonies. Quakers were instrumental in the founding of Pennsylvania and other colonies.

Friends United Meeting had approved sponsorship of our work at its fall board meeting. It was a challenge to expand our ministry in Cabrini-Green to include a commitment to the Society of Friends, a denomination of thousands of people with a distinctive history and theology. To make a membership commitment to a gathered body of believers called for a willingness to be held accountable by not only this group of members, but by the larger Religious Society of Friends. After one year of initial Meetings for Worship, our group of twenty individuals from the Fellowship of Friends was ready to be approved as a preparatory meeting. The Chicago Monthly Meeting on the South Side of Chicago had agreed to be our parent meeting.

On a beautiful June Sunday morning in 1982, we gathered together at the Chicago Monthly Meetinghouse. Following a time of worship, those from the Fellowship of Friends were asked to come to the front of the meetinghouse. We were publicly affirmed and welcomed into membership. The presiding clerk of the meeting signed membership certificates for all those present. Members of the Chicago Meeting came forward to shake our hands and give us a hug. The Chicago Fellowship of Friends was born. We were Quakers!

As the Fellowship of Friends grew, people caught the vision of this new direction and embraced it. Many of our first members were young people who had been a part of our high school outreach. One of these individuals was Tim.

Tim had been involved through contact at the high school. Since Steve assisted the athletic department of the local high school, he was a familiar face to the students. Often he sat with them as they ate their hamburgers and French fries at the cafeteria tables. He was fondly known by the teens as the "Dud Man" for his habit of telling one-line jokes. To initiate a conversation, Steve would slip out a piece of paper from his pocket which contained three jokes from his private library of joke books.

"Why was the Mama Flea so upset?" he quizzed his audience.

Groans and laughter erupted as the students groped to guess the punch line first.

"Because her children were going to the dogs!" Steve retorted.

These jokes became an avenue of establishing relationships with the teens.

One day as Steve began his weekly entertainment in the cafeteria, Tim, a junior student at the high school, reached into his blue jeans and removed several worn photographs.

"Do you recognize these pictures?" Tim asked Steve.

"Sure I do! These are pictures of Camp Wonderland in Wisconsin where I used to work!" Steve said with astonishment.

"Well, my mother and I went to camp there about eight years ago," Tim said pointing to their picture. "I thought you might be interested in seeing these photos."

As Steve looked at the photos, he could see the resemblance between the young boy of nine in the pictures and the teenager of seventeen who sat at the table before him. They talked together about their memories of camp and the experiences they had shared. With their relationship re-established, Steve continued to see Tim in the following weeks.

Shortly thereafter, Tim began attending the weekly meetings of the Fellowship of Friends with another teen from the high school, Gary. Tim had made a decision to follow Christ in his life and was seeking a group of Christians with which to have fellowship and receive further growth in his faith. Soon Tim was a faithful attender also at worship and Bible studies.

"I want you to pray for me," he would ask, "My old friends are criticizing me because I have changed. They call me 'church boy' when I refuse to go along with their worldly ways. My parents don't seem to understand what is going on in my life. I really love my friends and family. I wish they could share in my love of the Lord."

Tim's burden for evangelism also extended itself to other young people in the community. He became an active volunteer for the high school program and helped as a counselor for the children at camp.

"Is Tim coming with us on our trip?" the teens would ask.

Gifted with a deep, rich voice, Tim became a favorite in the choir. His sincere love for the Lord could easily be felt as he sang as a soloist.

"Precious Lord, take my hand, lead me on, help me stand, I am tired, I am weak, I am worn..."

Following high school graduation Tim worked as a cook at a nearby restaurant and remained actively involved in the Fellowship of Friends. He struggled to know the future direction he should take with his life.

"Tim, I've got great news for you!" Steve said joyously. "I just got a call from Friends Bible College, and they want to offer you a scholarship for their school."

"Great! I'd like more for my life than working in a restaurant. If I went to college, I'd even have a chance to sing with the college choir and get voice lessons," Tim said.

"You need to call them back immediately if you are going to take the scholarship," Steve prompted.

"Wait! There is so much I need to think about. How would I get the money to go to Kansas? Will I really be able to get good grades in college? This is such a big step," he said with hesitation in his voice.

"First, you need to decide if you want it, and everything else will fall into place," Steve said confidently.

Tim decided to make the phone call and step out in faith to attend a Christian college. Members of the Fellowship of Friends gathered money to buy his bus ticket to Kansas and joined together at the downtown bus station to wave goodbye to him.

Tim and other teens like him became the foundation of our new community of faith in Cabrini-Green known as the Chicago Fellowship of Friends. Yet not all teens were so easily convinced.

Two Lives — Two Stories

4

"I preached the Truth amongst them, directing them to the Lord Jesus Christ to be their teacher, and to the measure of His Spirit in themselves, by which they might be turned from darkness to light, and from the power of Satan unto God."

George Fox

"This young man is a danger to the society," the state's attorney declared.

The teenager hung his head as he stood before the judge's bench with his eyes fixed on the floor. In the silence you could hear him sigh, and his shoulders drooped a little more.

"At the age of fourteen he is already shooting people. This time the victim was only shot in the leg. Next time Patrick shoots, it could mean death for someone," the lawyer continued.

"He should be tried as an adult and sentenced. Then he would learn he cannot get away with such behavior. He would learn discipline."

As I listened to the prosecutor's argument, I almost believed

30

him. The picture he painted of Patrick seemed grim and hopeless. Then I looked at Patrick. He was still just a boy. He was only five feet, one inch in height, small, and skinny. I wondered what would have driven him to such violence.

"Patrick needs another chance, your Honor," the public defender pled.

"Our psychological testing reveals that he is extremely impressionable to his surroundings. He lives in Cabrini-Green with an alcoholic mother and an absent father. He lacks a positive environment," she argued. "If he is sentenced to jail he might only become more of a hardened criminal. He needs a new home environment where he can receive nurturing and another chance."

I glanced at Patrick's mother standing before the judge. She was a petite woman who seemed my age. Her eyes had an absent stare, and she seemed unaware of the derogatory comments being made about her.

Thud! The judge's gavel came down quick and heavy.

"The court hereby sentences Patrick to residential care under Steve and Marlene Pedigo until he is no longer a minor."

It was over so quickly. Not only was this my first experience in a trial court room, but now I was walking out the door with a young man who would become a son to us. Steve and I had been the difference between prison and freedom for Patrick.

As we walked down the long hallways of the Juvenile Court of Cook County, I said a prayer asking for strength and wisdom. I was taking another big step which would change my life. Finally, we reached the Release Department.

"Patrick, you've met Steve before, but I want you to meet Marlene. You are lucky that the courts dismissed the 702 (transfer hearing), which would have meant you would be tried in Adult Court. Now you will be able to stay with the Pedigos. You will now be accountable to them as well as me. One of the first guidelines of the court is that you will not go back to Cabrini-Green," his probation officer explained.

"I'm not goin' with them!" Patrick blurted out.

"Well, we can always go back into the courtroom and tell the judge your decision," the officer retorted.

Patrick suddenly turned and quickly disappeared down the staircase.

"Maybe we shouldn't take him," Steve said. "Perhaps this wasn't a good idea."

As we walked down to the Probation Office, Patrick's mother began to search the hallways for her son. Soon after we reached the office, Patrick and his mother appeared in the doorway.

"I'm sorry. I was just mad 'cause I was expectin' to go back to the neighborhood for a while," he said as his eyes again focused on his feet. "My mother said being placed with you would be a good idea."

"Well, the rules are still the same, and I don't want to see this happen again," said the probation officer.

Slowly we walked toward the car, and Steve began to make conversation with Patrick. The burst of anger we had seen displayed in the courtroom was gone. Now he appeared quiet and cooperative. I dismissed his earlier display of emotions to the grief of leaving home.

During the next few days we took him shopping for clothes. We taught him about personal hygiene and assigned him household chores. Steve enrolled him in a private Catholic school where he could get special attention, since he had missed seventh grade from truancy. He started to attend worship with us. Then the dream stage was over.

After living with us for nearly a year, Patrick began to change. People told us they had seen him in Cabrini-Green. He would tell us he was going somewhere else and sneak over there. There were outbreaks of anger and a fight at his grammar school. When we asked him what was bothering him, we would get his denial, "Nothing!" We suspected he was on drugs again.

The week after his graduation from eighth grade, Patrick was sitting on the front porch of our house eating watermelon.

"You need to clean up the seeds you are spitting on the step so they don't attract flies," I warned him.

"No way! You guys already try to boss me around! I'm not

doin' it!"

With a burst of anger he stood up defiantly and took off down the street.

Steve later found him in Cabrini and brought him back. He reported the incident to his probation officer and made arrangements for him to begin counseling with Juvenile Court. On the day of his counseling sessions there was a repeat performance.

"Come on, Patrick it is time to leave for counseling," Steve casually remarked as he headed for the door.

"I'm not going!" Patrick said.

"We already talked about this. You knew the appointment was for today. Why don't you want to go now?" Steve asked.

"I don't want to go, and I'm not goin'," Patrick's voice became more angry this time.

"Well, it has already been arranged with the courts. You need to go," Steve urged again.

Suddenly, Patrick stormed out of the house and slammed the door to return to the streets of Cabrini. He spent several weeks of that summer at home with his mother and gang friends. He was back to his old ways and got high nearly every day. We refused to keep chasing him.

Finally, he was picked up by the police. They took him to Juvenile Court where he again became repentant. He asked for another chance; we agreed to try again.

That year Patrick received a grant to attend Gordon Technical High School as a freshman; it was one of the most prestigious Catholic high schools in the city. His grades improved. He won a boxing trophy in competition and joined a basketball team with the local park district. It seemed things were going better.

One evening while we were sitting at the dinner table enjoying Patrick's favorite meal of pork chops, he began to share about his inward pain.

"Steve, do you think you could help my mother out? She needs a bed for my sisters," Patrick asked.

"Sure, I can look into it and see if we can get someone to give us a bed. Why are you so worried about it?" Steve probed.

"Well, I've kinda been looking after my brother and sisters since I'm the oldest. I never see my father unless he happens to be driving through Cabrini, and their fathers aren't around either. My mother's drunk so much she can't really look out for things," he explained.

"One time when I was younger she left me in charge of them, and our apartment caught on fire. I still feel real bad about how my brother, Immanuel, was so badly burned," he continued.

"Didn't all this pain at home make you want to get away from the house?" Steve asked.

"Yeah. I got tired of it and started to hang around with the gang in my building. They became like family to me. We did everything together. When I would get high with them I could forget it all. What they did seemed exciting and fun," Patrick answered.

"That's how you got into the shooting incident, right?" I probed.

"Well, one day after I got high, I had walked across the blacktop and saw this boy from another gang who had jumped on me. I wanted to get back at him, so I pulled out a gun and shot him," Patrick confided.

The picture of Patrick's past opened our eyes to the deep pain many of the young people in Cabrini-Green live with in their hearts.

The spring of his freshman year in high school Patrick started to again sneak into Cabrini. During the last week of school, he ran away to join the action of the streets. The pull was too strong.

When we lost Patrick to the life of the streets, we experienced the pain of parents who attempt to have tough love. At first we were in shock as we realized that the gang had succeeded in drawing him toward a life of repeated crime and slow suicide from drugs. We were angry because officials refused to stop the influx of drugs into our communities and country. We were depressed; even our best had not been good enough. We blamed ourselves and thought of ways we could have handled the situation differently. We experienced the pain of grief and failure.

When Patrick was eighteen he was arrested for theft. Upon his release he spent another few months with us. During this time he achieved his G.E.D. and his first full-time job at Pizza Hut. Yet the signs of his drug problem were still evident. That summer he spent large quantities of time in Cabrini and then quit his job. When we demanded that he receive drug counseling, he again left for the streets of Cabrini. Later he was arrested for theft and is now in the process of receiving counseling for his substance abuse through a court order. He now admits he has a serious drug problem and hopes to change his life upon release.

Our experience with Patrick pushed us to create a successful program for other children which would create an alternative to the negative community forces. Something other than drugs and organized gangs needed to fill their need for a sense of security and belonging. Through our Youthquake program, we provide a sense of community and support for young people. Activities include basketball teams, camping, monthly outings, and weekly group meetings. The weekly Youthquake gatherings begin with a time of singing, crowd breakers, a short devotional, and small group discussions about the evening's topic.

Peer pressure, sex, drugs, and other daily issues are discussed, and positive moral values are stressed. Youthquake becomes a place where teens can find positive peer support.

One of the teens whose life was changed was Calvin. Steve met Calvin through Youthquake and as coach of basketball at the high school. He seemed temperamental, yet distant. One day Calvin suddenly quit the high school basketball team because he thought Steve wasn't giving him enough time in the game. Steve tried to talk him out of the decision, but Calvin refused to reconsider. Later that summer, Steve was glad to see him agree to go to camp in Colorado.

"Just lean back and trust the rope," Steve encouraged from below.

"I'm too scared," Calvin yelled back.

It was a new experience to rappel down the cliff of one of Colorado's Rocky Mountains. This was not what he had thought camp would be like.

"It's a breeze," Sam added.

"Are you kidding? This mountain is tall," Calvin said in frustration.

Slowly he moved down the face of the mountain until he reached Steve at the bottom.

"Am I glad to see you. I thought I'd never make it to the bottom," Calvin sighed as he removed his harness.

"You did a good job! See, you can do it."

Calvin had been a part of the Young Friends program, and later he was on Steve's basketball team. He and other members of Youthquake had looked forward to camp as one of the highlights of the year. It was a chance to get away from the regular routine of life to reflect on one's life and draw closer to God. There were new experiences and new friends to enjoy.

Yet one tragic event was not in the plans.

"Steve, wake up! Did you hear the news? One of the counselors has been struck by lightning!"

Steve's quiet nap alone in the cabin during a storm was suddenly interrupted by the tragic news.

"Let's get the guys together and talk," Steve suggested.

Minutes later the boys climbed onto their bunk beds in the cabin. In shock, their faces had a blank look as they solemnly stared up towards the ceiling.

"What do you feel about what happened?" Steve asked.

"I never thought death would happen out here. We left Cabrini to get away from this."

"Goes to show it goes with you wherever you go."

"We can't escape reality. The real question is how you deal with death," Steve continued.

"Some people try to ignore it."

"Some people try to forget it."

"Some people try to think it will never happen to them."

"You know you don't need to be afraid of death if your life is in Christ's hands. I want to show you something about God you need to know," Steve responded as he reached for a small tract written by Billy Graham.

Together they read the tract, and moments later they prayed to commit their lives to Christ. A feeling of peace existed as they walked out together to wait for dinner.

It was this inner peace from Christ which Calvin took back with him to Cabrini-Green. That fall the basketball coaches commented that he seemed to have more patience. Calvin even commented to others on Steve's good coaching. He began to attend special tutoring at the high school so his grades would improve. His mother and brother began to come regularly to worship.

"We started to notice positive changes in Calvin's life. He even began to tell me what was right and wrong. I wanted to come and find out more about the Fellowship of Friends," his mother told us.

Then one spring on Easter Sunday Calvin stepped forward to take the right hand of membership from the Fellowship of Friends. We rejoiced! One more teenager was convinced of the truth of Christ Jesus and the need to live as a witness to it in the Cabrini-Green community. We heard the inward voice of the Lord calling us to continue in ministry to reach out in love to those "Patricks" and "Calvins" which surrounded us.

A
New Home

5

*"True religion does not draw men out of the
world but enables them to live better in it and
excites their endeavors to mend it."*

William Penn

"We really need a place of our own in Cabrini," I dreamed.
January's bitterly cold wind blew against the back of my coat
as we tried to connect the battery cables from our car to the
stalled van. The old 1977 van was filled with high school teens
waiting for a ride to our Wednesday evening meeting.

As I climbed into the driver's seat behind the frosty windows,
I reached for the key. The engine uttered a few faint spurts and
fell silent. My heart sank. The image of tow trucks, repair bills,
and hauling kids in our car was not a welcome thought.

Minutes later the first six of us squeezed into our small
Chevette to get a ride to the meeting. Other volunteers began to
help us transport the teens with their cars, too. The old van and
its problems became a painful joke among us.

Our transportation problems had heightened due to the
increased growth in our programs. Lisa Johanon, a graduate of

nearby Moody Bible Institute, had developed the Young Friends ministry to include seventy-five grade-school children in the weekly programs. Young Friends focused upon three learning centers: recreation, Bible stories, and arts and crafts. Weekly the children gathered to sit around Lisa in a semi-circle as she placed figures on a flannel board to tell the Bible story. Later she would challenge them to memorize a Bible verse which related to the story. She gave rewards to those who memorized scripture passages and who had good attendance records. Lisa also took the children on monthly outings and summer camping trips. The children loved Young Friends and Lisa!

In addition to her activities with the children, Lisa visited weekly in homes and helped us to make new contacts with several parents in the community. Her leadership and later that of her husband, Dan Johanon, greatly increased the ministry of the Fellowship of Friends.

This program expansion also meant we needed to locate additional space. We started to transport young people for their programs to rented space at the Gospel League of Chicago, an emergency-care facility for women. We used the basement of a nearby church Sunday afternoons for worship. Our home remained the site for Bible studies and choir practice. Coordinating transportation for one hundred people to various sites in our old vans and keeping up with the continual repairs also had become a major task. Besides the inconvenience, we lacked unity between the different groups who used various sites.

That summer I prayed the Lord would give us our own place in Cabrini. I called for options.

"Our rental price is $1,200 per month."

"Our facilities are for office use only."

"It's not for rent; it's for sale at $450,000!"

Since Cabrini-Green is only blocks away from Chicago's business "Loop" and the Gold Coast, it was going to be difficult to find something within our budget. I swallowed hard at the news I heard over the telephone. Somehow I knew the Lord would make a way, and I continued to pray.

Then I thought of the Archdiocese of Chicago. They had several parishes on the Near North Side. I gave them a call.

"I'm sorry, we do not lease facilities. However, we do have a building to sell, St. Phillips on Oak Street."

My mind flashed to the St. Phillips location. It was on the corner of Oak and Cambridge Streets, centrally located in Cabrini-Green and on the edge of two gang turfs. With two floors of classrooms and a large basement, it had ample space for our programs. It seemed ideal.

After weeks of negotiation, we signed the deed to the property on November 5, 1982, with another Christian organization, CYCLE (Community Youth Creative Learning Experience). St. Phillips had been scheduled for demolition that fall, but now it would again become a center of activity for the children of Cabrini.

I can still remember the first time I walked down the hallways of the building.

"Steve, look at all the room in this building," I said excitedly as we walked down the first-floor hallway.

"Come in here, Marlene," Steve urged.

As I walked into one of the classrooms, the chipped paint from the walls and ceiling cracked underneath my feet. Then I noticed the wall before me. Countless cracks and fallen plaster gave a grim warning to any would-be renovators.

"There must be a horrible roof; look at all the water damage on this wall," Steve pointed out.

"Oh, no!" I wailed.

"And look at the windows which will need to be replaced," Steve said as he pointed at the glass which had been shattered by a bullet.

"It is going to cost a lot of money to fix this old thing up," said a friend who had come along to give advice.

"It's going to take work, too. Look at the layers of dust on everything. You can tell it hasn't been used in a while," Steve continued.

"But once you get it cleaned and painted, it will look completely different. I know we can do it!" I encouraged them.

The first winter we drained the pipes and let our sleeping giant sit while we prepared for its renovation. I began to search through the Donor's Forum Library for potential sources of funding and sent out proposals. We wrote letters appealing for volunteers who would help us begin the renovation in the spring. We found a friend, Phil, who was willing to help coordinate our work crews and renovation.

One evening Steve and I visited Mrs. Johnson and her friend for a time of Bible study and prayer. Mrs. Johnson's son, Gary, actively attended our meetings with his friend, Tim. His mother loved the Lord and was always a source of encouragement to us.

"Mrs. Johnson, the architects have told us it will take $250,000 to renovate our building, and we only have a few thousand in the bank. We need a miracle!" I explained.

"Well, the Lord is the one who specializes in miracles. All we have to do is pray," she said with assurance.

That evening as we sat around her kitchen table, we turned our hearts toward the Lord in prayer.

"Lord, you know we have come this far in faith. You are the one who owns the cattle on a thousand hills. We have done all we can possibly do to prepare for the renovation of the building. Now we really need the finances and volunteers to make it a reality," I prayed.

"Lord, we just want to thank you for all you have done for us. We know you are a mighty big God and nothing is too hard for you. We just know you will make a way somehow for this building to be used for your ministry. Thank you, Jesus." Mrs. Johnson's face seemed to radiate her faith and confidence.

We gave her a hug and climbed up the steps towards her door.

"Now, don't worry. It's all in God's hands," she reminded us.

I left full of peace.

Just a few weeks later, we received a check in the mail for $25,000 from the McCormick Charitable Trust! Now we knew we could begin the renovation in the spring.

That next year Phil coordinated volunteers from not only the Cabrini community, but from across the country. Our work crews came from Friends Bible College in Kansas; Iowa Yearly Meeting of Friends; Marion, Indiana Friends Church; Friends Disaster Service in Ohio; Western Yearly Meeting; Muscatine, Iowa Friends Church; North Carolina Yearly Meeting Youth Group; Chicago Monthly Meeting; the Chicago General Meeting of Friends; and the Quaker International Youth Pilgrimage which included teens from across the world. Some groups even came more than once. Other groups also came through CYCLE. Slowly, the building was transformed by the efforts of many.

"Pass me that other sledge hammer, John," Steve said.

"Sure thing," the young man said as he stopped work to hand Steve the hammer.

An active part of the Fellowship of Friends, John had introduced his cousin, William, to the high school program, too. They had come that day to help Steve knock down a wall in the basement of the building.

"Hey, Arab, when you gonna take that towel off your head?" William teased as he loaded the wheelbarrow with additional bricks.

"I'm just protectin' my beautiful head of hair, chump," John replied.

"Those goggles are sure 'jay' too!" William continued as he took his load toward the doorway to empty in the dumpster outside the door.

As the wall came down, the dumpster filled up.

"I think you guys need a break," I said interrupting their work, "Why don't you stop for some lemonade and hot dogs?"

"Sure sounds fine to me," Steve said, "My back is starting to kill me."

"It's time to quit, anyway. The bricks are starting to fall off the sides of the dumpster, it's so full," William said.

I always made refreshments for the volunteers at home and then took them to the building in our car. Everyone seemed to work up an appetite and thirst when they helped. As Steve and the teens removed their gloves and goggles to wash up, I poured everyone a large glass of ice-cold lemonade.

"Get out of here, man," John shouted as he ran through the room. His hair was dripping with water.

"I'm just trying to help you clean up," said William as he chased after him with another cup of water.

"It's been a long hot day in this basement. I think we're ready to quit," said Steve, smiling as he reached for a glass of lemonade.

"Come on, guys. Let's thank the Lord for this food and eat." After the blessing, they began to devour the hot dogs.

"Did you see the wall Steve and I tore down today?" John asked.

"Did you see the dumpster is full of all the bricks I carried out there?" William added.

"These guys did a great job," Steve said as he put his arm around John's shoulder. Large grins spread across John's and William's faces.

As we ate, I realized there would be other benefits from our working together that year than just seeing the building renovated.

As the weeks passed we repaired one room in the building after another. Our greatest test of imagination came in making a dark, damp, vacant room in the basement into a kitchen. After removing a broken pool table from the room and scrubbing every inch of space, we painted it a bright sky blue with white trim.

Next, Lisa and I bought kitchen cabinets for $100 from a sale of used furniture at the Illinois Masonic Hospital where her husband, Dan, worked. The cabinets, which had been painted yellow, green, and blue, and used to store medical supplies, now were repainted white and hung on the wall to hold our pots and pans. Our counter tops and kitchen island came from used office furniture no longer needed when the Chicago Board of Trade decided to move into their new offices. Old stoves and refrigerators were found in alleys or donated by friends. The red ceramic kitchen floor tiles came from the Community Renewal Corporate Donations Warehouse. A carpenter from Chicago Monthly Meeting came to install a window in the wall to provide a serving area into the next room. Finally, Western Yearly Meeting of Friends donated $5,000 to install a kitchen ventilation system to bring the room up to Chicago City Code standards. With hard work and ingenuity, the transformation continued throughout the building.

One of the most memorable work crews was the Quaker Youth Pilgrimage, a group of thirty teens from Quaker meetings across the world. During their four-week visit to the United States, they spent a few days helping us with the renovation.

"How in the world do these scaffolds work?" asked a young man from Canada as he looked at the pile of pipes and boards lying on the floor.

"Here, let me show you," said William as he quickly arranged the pipes into a stand and shoved the board across the top to create a place to work for the would-be painters.

"How do I look?" asked the teenager from Jamaica as she climbed to the top of the scaffold with a paint brush in hand.

"Great!" we all cheered.

"I think lime green with white trim would look good on these walls. Can you mix up that color of paint, Phil?" asked a beautiful young girl from Philadelphia.

In the meantime I had gathered a group in the adjoining room to begin plastering the cracks in the wall, the result of water damage because a softball was left in the drain pipes for too long.

"This is how you mix up plaster," I explained from my months of experience.

"I've plastered before at home," one young man from Indiana said proudly.

"Good, am I glad to see you! You can be in charge of this plastering group," I smiled with relief.

In another room they began the process of scraping the old peeling paint from the walls.

"You need to wear these goggles and get a hat or towel for your head," Fred told the novices in the group.

"Oh, no, I just broke a fingernail," wailed a young girl from

London as she scraped the putty knife along the chipped paint.

"Wait 'til the end of the day," teased William.

By the end of the day the effects of their hard work was obvious to us all. Good feelings and a spirit of togetherness had developed. After eating hot dogs at the lakefront, there was a time of singing and sharing among these young people from a variety of countries, classes, and races. More than the building was built that day.

After nearly a year of renovation, we gathered together on a Sunday morning in April, 1984, to dedicate the building to the Lord. With more than two hundred people present for the ceremony, we recognized the efforts of countless volunteers who gave thousands of hours of volunteer labor to the project. Their labors of love had helped us complete the project for less than $50,000 when we had been told it would be $250,000. We read the names of donors who had contributed the financial resources which provided the materials we used. Their caring was a blessing from the Lord.

Mayor Harold Washington spoke words of encouragement for groups such as ours who were willing to work hard for their community. Other community leaders affirmed their support for our programs and their appreciation for our transforming the building for expanded use in the community. We lifted our hearts in praise to the Lord for his blessing and asked that the building would become a haven of peace and a witness of God's love in Cabrini-Green.

Street
Life

6

"It has been well said that 'earthly cares are heavenly discipline.' But they are even something better than discipline — they are God's chariots, sent to take the soul to its high places of triumph."
Hannah Whitall Smith

"Darryl just called. His friend has been killed, and Darryl's been arrested. I'm going to the police station," Steve said as he awakened me.

"Do you have to go? It's one o'clock in the morning, and it's below zero. The car probably won't even start," I said sleepily.

"I'm gone," Steve replied as he finished tying his shoe strings and left.

As I heard the door close behind him, I finally jolted awake. Then I remembered what Darryl had told Steve Sunday at church.

"The gang is trying to kill me, Steve."

"What happened?" Steve had asked.

"Well, I was waiting to go to work at the bus stop and one of the gang members came up to me and stuck a gun inside my

46

coat. He shot a bullet through the back part of my coat," Darryl had explained.

"I thought they were going to leave you alone. They've already shot you once in the foot. Why don't you come over to the house and stay for a while until things have calmed down," Steve had offered.

"Let me try one more thing. I'm going to meet with the gang leader this afternoon and see if I can work something out so it will all stop. I don't really want to leave my family."

We were worried for him. Darryl had been involved in the gang at an early age. When he was dismissed from a local high school for the possession of a gun, Steve began working with him through Juvenile Court. Darryl became active in the Fellowship of Friends, and Steve helped him to enroll in a Christian alternative high school where his grades improved until he was on the honor roll. He got a job working nearly full time after school at a convenience store. Darryl was interviewed by a reporter about his success story. His mistake, however, was he did not take the gang seriously.

"Darryl has been charged with murder," Steve said when he returned home.

"You've got to be kidding! What happened?"

"Before he had to be at work, he dropped by the home of his boss, Frank. Two gang members were with him. As Darryl was talking to Frank, the gang members went into the washroom and came out with their guns pulled. They wanted to rob Frank and his friends, but they didn't have large amounts of money in the house. Thinking they weren't really telling the truth, the gang members had Frank and his friends tied and began to torture them to tell where they kept their money. They tried to force Darryl at gunpoint to kill one of Frank's friends with a knife, but Darryl only wounded him. Then the gang members killed Frank and fled. Darryl ran to a police car for help. The officers told him to dial 911. After the call, Darryl came back to the house to wait for them. When the police arrived, they arrested Darryl," Steve explained.

"What is going to happen? Aren't they going to let Darryl go?

48

Wasn't he a victim, too?" I asked.

"It doesn't look good. Frank and his friends are white. The gang probably set Darryl up to take the rap because he wanted out of the gang. We should have insisted Darryl come and stay with us," Steve said in frustration.

Steve was right. The jury found Darryl guilty. He was sent to prison where gang members tried to kill him. After being isolated in a special ward, Darryl finally adjusted. He began to pray and read the Bible. He started to take college courses and got a job in the cafeteria. He now waits for a retrial and hopes he will not have to spend the next twenty years of his life in jail.

"It's only the Lord who is helping me get through all of this," Darryl writes.

Living the Christian life is not always easy in Cabrini-Green. Temptation and danger surround the young people daily.

"Someone's throwing something," James, age eight, said as the car window in the parking lot shattered.

"No, man, they're shooting at me," Raymond, age ten, said as a bullet rushed under his nose.

Raymond and his friend, James, had walked around the back of their Cabrini-Green highrise to find Raymond's uncle who had planned to work under the hood of his disabled Nova. Rather than finding him, they had walked into trouble.

"Quick, let's get out of here."

The boys sprinted to the entrance of their apartment building and turned to discover who their assailant might be. However, not yet out of danger, James felt a bullet enter his right calf.

"Ahhh! I've been shot," James exclaimed as he bent over with pain.

Within seconds Raymond darted to the lobby to locate the security guards.

"My friend's been shot!"

"Quit playing."

"For real, he needs help."

"Get out of here."

By then James had limped to the elevator to take him to the

fifth floor. Raymond raced up the stairs to James' house as the screen door slammed behind him.

"James has been shot," Raymond shouted.

"Quit playing, Raymond," James' mother scolded.

Then she noticed James out of the corner of her eye staggering at the doorway.

"Stop crying and panicking," she said as she held him close to soothe him.

Within minutes James' stepbrother had carried him downstairs to a car to rush him to the hospital. The bullet was too close to the bone; the doctors were unable to remove it.

Their assailant, they found out, had been the older brother of someone with whom Raymond had fought. They had been aiming for Raymond and had shot James by mistake.

"You'd better get your life right with the Lord," Raymond's mother said as she shared with him about Christ, "you've got to stop doing these bad things."

"She's right," James said, "there needs to be a change in my life, too. We've been doing what we know is bad just to be accepted by our friends."

Through the ministry of Lisa, Raymond and James began attending Young Friends regularly. They began to learn more about God. A change in their lives began to occur.

When they became a part of the Junior High Young Friends, their involvement deepened. Besides the regular meetings, they attended outings, rallies, camping trips, and were members of the softball team. James and Raymond helped renovate the building. One Saturday the Quaker men from a work crew taught them how to hammer new floor boards. They also volunteered to tear down walls and take turns with the wheelbarrow as the bricks were sent to the dumpster. Their faith and sense of community grew. While boys in their building joined a gang, they attended membership classes to make a commitment to the church. They became friends with Sam, another young man their age from the turf of a rival gang.

"Does Sam live here?" the officer said at two o'clock one morning at the door to one of the Cabrini apartments.

50

"No," was the quick response from the young man of ten who stood before them.

"Sam, what they want?" came the voice of a young woman in the back bedroom.

"Are you Sam?"

"Yeah."

"We have to take you to the police station."

Once in the police station, they reviewed Sam's pranks which occurred earlier that day.

"We've been told you pulled the fire alarm six times today at school," the officer charged.

"I was mad at my teacher," Sam retorted.

"You've also been picked up several times for curfew violation, stealing from Montgomery Ward and trying to jump the 'el' for a free ride," the officer continued.

"All my friends do it."

"Well, you'd better start doing better or you'll wind up in jail," the officer warned.

Sam began to think about his life and his future. He had heard stories about jail from his two older brothers who had been there. Then he began to notice his friends were getting too bold as thieves. He knew they were getting real police records. Even his mother urged him to go back to the church he occasionally attended earlier.

When he started to attend Young Friends, his friends made fun of him. However, he found himself drawn toward the friendly people he met who made him feel important. One night at a rally, he committed his life to Christ, and he started to change. Soon he was a regular attender for worship where he enjoyed the choir and sermons. When Sam was asked to become a member, he responded.

The commitment of Quakers to peace and working toward making the world better was what he believed, too. Within his heart grew the feeling of responsibility that he needed to become more active to spread this good news.

"Did you hear that Leroy was shot?" Gerald asked his friend as they sat on the hood of the car outside of their apartment building.

"Why don't you talk about good stuff and not always about

gang banging," Sam challenged him.

"Shut up," Gerald snapped.

"Why would you become a gang banger (member)?" Sam continued.

"Because I keep getting jumped on, and I want my revenge," another friend added.

"I've been jumped on, too. Remember when I got beat with a stick by Floyd? Remember when I got my head busted with a brick on Hudson Playground? I had to have seven stitches," Sam added.

"Yeah."

"Remember when those gang members stole my groceries? I just want to forget about those times, and so should you," Sam urged.

"Go tell the older gang bangers that," one of the younger boys responded.

"They're already grown, and I can't tell them anything. I am trying to tell you," Sam warned.

"You don't have to listen to that church boy," one of the older gang members hollered. He had been standing against the entrance to the building listening to their conversation.

"Come here!"

Obediently the younger boys got up from the hood of the car to find out what he wanted.

"Why are you going?" Sam asked.

"We have to see what he wants," they replied and they left Sam sitting on the car alone.

Yet, Sam continues his effort to reach the hearts of younger people with the message of Christ. He serves as a volunteer for all three youth programs: Young Friends (K-6), Junior High Young Friends (7-8), and Youthquake. Through the songs he sings in the choir, he witnesses of the faith he holds dearly. As an active member of the Outreach Committee, he joins others from the church to discuss the problems of the community and possible solutions. He dreams of the day when more people in Cabrini-Green will come to know Christ and stand up for peace in the community.

Claiming Quaker Identity

7

> *"In the Eternal Now all men become seen in a new way. We enfold them in our love, and we and they are enfolded together within the great Love of God as we know it in Christ."*
>
> Thomas R. Kelly

"I'm looking for God," the young woman said simply.

Steve was standing on the sidewalk outside the meeting-house greeting people as they came to worship. He was surprised to be approached by the older sister of one of the students he had known at the high school.

"Well, come on in, Charlotte. God will be here this morning," Steve said as he warmly shook her hand and invited her and Darius, her son, up the stairs.

As we quieted our hearts for worship, I noticed the new attenders sitting in one of the back rows.

"Lord, please bless this woman and her son. Meet the needs of their hearts today," I prayed silently.

"I'm gonna lay down my burden... down by the riverside," the choir sang with conviction.

52

Throughout worship, I noticed our guests listened carefully to the scripture and sermon. In the closing moments of the open worship I heard Charlotte pray.

"Lord, just bless all those who could not make it today. I want to ask you for guidance and protection for my son and myself. I also want to say a prayer for my mother and family. Bless them, too. Lord, just give me peace in my life and my family."

As she spoke I could hear the quiet pain of a broken heart before the Lord. I knew she had found God.

When I met Charlotte after worship, I learned she was a student at Chicago State University and lived just down the street. She offered to help me that following week with my office work so she might gain work experience. I quickly accepted her offer.

When she came into the office that week I asked her to help me coordinate the mailing list of the participants in the Fellowship of Friends. As we updated phone numbers and addresses I asked, "What brought you to the Fellowship of Friends?"

"Well, I had gone to see my father in Ohio, and one of my relatives encouraged me to get involved in a church. Then on the way home a complete stranger on the bus gave me the same message. I started to think I needed to find God in my life," she explained.

"But why the Fellowship of Friends?" I persisted.

"A long time ago Steve said something to me which I have never forgotten. When I was attending the YMCA College downtown he said he was proud of my getting an education. Then he said, 'Don't forget to bring what you learn back into the community.' I have never forgotten that."

"I'm glad you didn't! It's good to have you as a part of the Fellowship of Friends. I really appreciate all the help you've given me today," I said as I put my arm around her shoulders.

Throughout the following weeks our friendship developed. That fall Charlotte and Darius attended our church retreat, and shortly afterwards Charlotte announced that she was no longer taking any drugs. We rejoiced in her victory.

Charlotte began to volunteer with Young Friends that year,

and Darius became an active attender at the Junior High Young Friends. I noticed the deep love she had for the children with whom she worked. She even started to bring her friends to worship. With glad hearts we accepted her into membership of the Fellowship of Friends on Christmas Sunday.

Other adults slowly became active in the Fellowship of Friends. One woman who would quickly become a "mother" for our church was Mary Ann. One day after worship, she invited several adults from the Fellowship of Friends to her home for dinner.

When I first walked into her Cabrini apartment, my eyes were drawn to her kitchen table laden with an incredible feast: fried chicken, fresh collard greens, corn bread, potato salad, tossed salad, green beans, and iced tea! After the blessing we filled our plates and began to share about experiences which brought us to the Fellowship of Friends.

"I came to the Fellowship of Friends to find a church where I wasn't just a part of a crowd. One church I attended only seemed concerned about the money I gave and if I would support the pastor. I'm tired of those experiences. I knew about the Fellowship of Friends because of Steve, Marlene, and Barb," Mary Ann began.

"My son, Fred, went to camp with Steve as a teenager. Steve also helped my other son, Lonny, to get a job as a runner at an advertising agency. Then Barb, one of the elders of the church, always seemed to be there to listen and help when I needed her. I started to think I should try the church," Mary Ann continued.

"Fellowship of Friends gave me an opportunity to help others," Barb explained. "I had felt called to become more involved in the problems of the city and didn't really know how to begin. Then I met Marlene, and she invited me to volunteer with the high school ministry. Since then I've taken kids to camp, helped with Youthquake meetings, led a drama group, and have been an elder of the church. I'm one of the charter members of the Fellowship of Friends."

"I've changed in so many ways since I've come to the Fellowship of Friends," Charlotte added. "One small area is that God has helped me to speak first and smile to people on the street who don't normally speak. I also enjoy the women's Bible study we have on Thursday mornings."

"That's been a source of encouragement for me, too," Mary Ann affirmed. "We are having a great time reading about the various women of the Bible. We also pray for each other's problems and concerns."

As the afternoon drew to a close, we thanked Mary Ann for her warm hospitality and the wonderful meal. I could sense the loving fellowship of the adults who were starting to become active. Our circle of friends continued to grow.

"Hello, I am interested in attending a Friends meeting. Can you tell me what time worship is held?" the young woman's voice said over the phone late one Saturday evening.

"We would love to have you. Worship begins at 11:00 a.m." Steve replied.

The next morning as the choir sang during worship, I noticed a young couple about our age walk into the room with their two daughters.

"The Lord wants you to use your gifts to serve the Kingdom of God," Steve preached. "So many young people grow up and later forget where they are from. They only think about getting a job, making money, and their own pleasures. This community needs people to put their lives together and then make a commitment to help others do the same thing. God blesses us so that we might help those in need around us."

During the open worship the husband rose to his feet, "I really didn't want to come here this morning. This was all my wife's idea. However, this sermon was meant for me. I grew up in the Henry Horner Housing Development on the West Side and have become successful in the music industry. Since our marriage we have never been able to find a church where we both felt comfortable about making a commitment. I am impressed with what you are doing and all the young people that are here today. Now I am glad we came."

After worship Steve and I went up and introduced ourselves.

"I'm so glad you came this morning. How did you discover

the Fellowship of Friends?"

"I had been reading about various denominations and I came across the Religious Society of Friends. As I read more about the Quakers I said, 'This is what I believe. Where is this church?'" Joan said.

"I began looking in the telephone book to discover if I would find a Quaker church. First, I called the meeting closest to us in Oak Park. They told us about the Fellowship of Friends and suggested that we might wish to attend," she continued.

"We're so glad you came. Did you have any trouble finding us?" Steve asked.

"I am a speech therapist and I often come to Cabrini to provide services for the day-care centers. We didn't have any problems getting here," Joan replied.

"This is my husband, Jun, and my two daughters, Season and Carson."

"Come over to our home this week for an early morning breakfast of waffles, and we can tell you more about the church and what we are doing," Steve invited.

"Sounds great to me!" Jun responded.

During the following weeks they continued to come and later became members. Joan's communications gifts became a great asset to the Fellowship of Friends as she presided over our business sessions and helped us work through difficult issues to find consensus. She can handle tough situations and help members of the meeting listen to each other's needs.

Joan expressed deep appreciation for the Quaker process of business. Many black churches they had visited seemed to be primarily governed by the black pastor. Quaker business procedure empowers individual members to express their opinions and to use their talents for the Lord's service. She asked us several tough questions.

"Although Quakers were in the forefront of the abolition movement in the country, why are there not more black members in their meetings?"

"Why is it so difficult to find out what Quakers believe?"

"Isn't it time to tell the secret of Quakerism to the black

Chicago Fellowship of Friends

Above: Marlene Pedigo welcomes arrivals at the dedication of the renovated building in 1984.

Left: Chicago Mayor Harold Washington addresses the congregation at the dedication.

Below: Chicago Fellowship of Friends Meetinghouse at 515 West Oak Street.

Young Friends

Top: Debbie Davis from Moody Bible Institute helps junior high Young Friends make puppets.

Middle: Moody Bible Institute student, Lori Rogers, assists with a Young Friends 4-H cooking project.

Below: High rise city housing units border the neighborhood playground.

Away from the City

Right: A visit to Iowa gives an introduction to farm life.

Below: Boating is just one popular activity when Chicago Fellowship of Friends members go to Quaker Haven Camp, near North Webster, Indiana.

Worship, Study, Fellowship

Top: The Chicago Fellowship of Friends Choir adds an important element to worship.

Right: Steve Pedigo (l) and Peter Sjoblom from C.U.R.E. (r) join in Youthquake high schoolers' fun.

Below: Study is an important part of the Chicago Fellowship of Friends program.

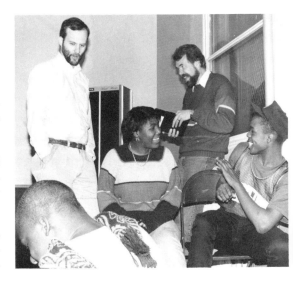

community in this country?"

Increased growth in the Fellowship of Friends programs and new adult attenders also brought with it growing pains as a church. Our transition from simply being a youth ministry into the deeper commitment of maintaining a church was difficult for some. Although some churches are completely managed by the clergy or a small group of people, the Quakers are not. Responsibility is placed upon all members to become active in decision-making, ministry and outreach. Some individuals were not ready to make this deeper commitment, even though they had been active as recipients of the youth ministry.

Others wanted to remain a club or clique rather than embracing the mission of a church to reach out to new people or those in need. This is natural for teenagers who are seeking an identifiable peer group of which to be a part. A group spirit and pride develops for "their group." However, this spirit which may be normal for teenagers cannot be the basis of a mature church. A healthy church must see its mission not merely to its membership, but also to include an outreach to others, to evangelism. If our congregation were focused inward upon itself, there would be no growth, and a "Quaker Club" would develop rather than a church. It was heart-breaking for us to realize some of the young people with whom we had worked did not want to make a commitment to a church and grow deeper in their faith.

Other individuals tested the Fellowship of Friends to see if we would really be a Quaker church. A young man broke the silence of our open worship one Sunday morning with these words: "I have been fasting for three days, and I want to rebuke this church and its teachings."

I cringed in my chair. My eyes glanced at Steve to see his reaction. I wondered what he was thinking. We had never experienced anyone taking the silence of our open worship to rebuke another person, let alone to hear criticism of the church.

"You should dress appropriately when you come to church. You come to honor God on Sundays."

For nearly fifteen minutes he continued with his rebuke

before sitting down. After the worship service, Steve called together the members of the church to discuss the situation.

"When we became members of the Fellowship of Friends we made a commitment to the larger Religious Society of Friends. One of the testimonies of Quakers is their commitment to simplicity. What is most important to God is our heart and how we respond obediently to the Spirit of the Lord. Since Christ's spirit is alive in our hearts every day of the week, Sunday does not need to be a special day to dress. God is not just in this building," Steve explained.

Others began to voice their opinion in support of simplicity.

"I like the fact that I don't have to wear fancy clothes to come to church. A lot of people dress up for church, and after they leave they live like the Devil the rest of the week. It doesn't change their hearts."

"I don't have the money to buy expensive dresses and hats anyway. I just have my blue jeans which I wear to school. If we did that I'd have to stay home from church."

"I think the important thing is that you dress modestly and not to flirt. You should dress that way every day."

"The early Quakers developed simplicity as a testimony against people in their society who put their focus on acquiring material things rather than upon their Creator who made them," I said. "That is why our church does not spend money on fancy candlesticks, crosses, windows, or other elaborate decorations. Our money needs to be spent to further God's Kingdom. In the same way, we do not need to spend money on fancy clothes to impress God. We can use our resources for others. The early Quakers dressed in grey and black for this reason. Although we do not need to become legalistic about dress codes, we need to remember our testimony of simplicity."

"I like the fact that Steve doesn't wear a suit. Sometimes you look at a minister's clothes and car and you think all of the church's money is going into his pocket."

"Those are the churches that often beg their poor members for money, too."

"I guess that is one of the things which separates us from the other churches."

The elders met that Sunday evening to discuss how to handle the situation. It was agreed that we would contact our critic and ask to speak with him individually about the issue. However, when he was called on the phone, he said he did not want to meet. After his confrontation he never came back.

We also decided to implement a ten-week series for all individuals who might be interested in becoming a member of the Fellowship of Friends. This membership class was to educate individuals about the testimonies of Friends and their biblical basis. Our clearness about Quakerism would hopefully help alleviate future conflict situations and better equip members to communicate to others about their faith.

Although it was hard to hear the words of rebuke, it was a turning point for the Fellowship of Friends. Our test to see if we would remain true to the testimony of simplicity led to our greater identification as Quakers. One more step was taken towards the development of our bond together as a church.

Nurturing
Leadership

8

"... the Church is meant to be an incendiary fellowship and nothing less."

D. Elton Trueblood

"How many people served as volunteers this past week?"

A dozen teens in my Sunday School class sat around a table in folding chairs with eager anticipation on their faces to report their activities. After their response, Altamease took a red marker and put a point next to their names on a large chart. Each point meant they were closer to attending summer camp in North Carolina.

"I helped to teach the Young Friends lesson to the children this week. Even though those kids get on my nerves when they don't listen, I think I did a good job teaching them," reported Gloria.

"Would you believe I called Brian up and asked if I could wash the van this week?" James smiled. "You should have seen the van — it was a mess before we cleaned it. There were candy wrappers on the floor and dirt all over. Now it almost looks new!"

"I led a skit for the high school Youthquake meeting this week. We did a role play where I pretended to rob someone. Then we stopped the action to ask the audience if they would 'trick' on me for robbing. At first everyone laughed, but then we got down to talking about it seriously. They liked my skit," Sam said proudly.

"Sam has volunteered so much he already has enough points to go to North Carolina," Altamease reported.

"That's because he almost lives at the Fellowship of Friends," Darius laughed.

Other teens also reported their volunteer work. Theodore, a budding artist, had helped Charlotte in the arts and crafts room with Young Friends. Altamease, a very good listener, had served as a small-group counselor for the Junior High Young Friends. Robert, who loved music, had led group singing for the high school Youthquake program.

"Some of you need to get busy or you won't be going to North Carolina with us this summer," Altamease teased.

"Is there something I can do this week to get more points?" Calvin asked.

"I need more points, too," Bev said.

"I'm sure we can think of something," I smiled.

I looked around the table at the high schoolers before me. Many of them had grown up in our Young Friends program and early in their lives had made a commitment to Christ. Their participation in the program had created a strong, positive peer group. Now they were actively involved in the ministry of the Fellowship of Friends as positive role models for the younger children. They had caught the vision of what it means to be a servant of Christ Jesus.

The vision had spread to other members of the Fellowship of Friends, too. Each week I helped to lead the Junior High Young Friends program. One of our most committed volunteer counselors was Karoline. As a teen in Cabrini, Karoline had been an active member of the Fellowship of Friends. She regularly sang in the choir, served as our recording clerk, and attended weekly Koinonia groups. Even though she was now a full-time student at Northeastern University, she still found time to volunteer with the Young Friends program. One particular evening her lesson from James encouraged her group to control their tongues so they could live as peacemakers. I wondered how she would teach this difficult concept.

"We can help to bring peace to our community if we can learn to control our tongues," Karoline said as an introduction to the topic.

"What is wrong with 'casing?' Everyone does it."

"I'm just playing when I talk about other people. It is only when someone talks about my mother that I start to get upset."

"When someone tries to 'bus' on you, what can you do?"

"You are asking some tough questions. Maybe it would help if we could role play different ways we could respond to someone who wants to be negative," Karoline suggested.

The girls pushed back the tables and chairs in their room to create space for the stage. They decided to act out a scene where one girl tried to start a fight. After assigning parts, the play began.

"Come on, let's throw down big-headed Karoline," Tiffany challenged as she walked up to Karoline's face.

"I thought we were good friends. Why are you acting this way?" Karoline responded.

"You've never been my friend. You've been talking behind my back," Tiffany sneered.

"You have been listening to gossip again. I don't want to fight you. I think we should sit down and talk," Karoline replied.

Karoline and Tiffany sat down in two chairs and began to talk about the problem. Soon they were friends again. This role play led to further scenes which portrayed other daily conflict situations in the community.

"What did you learn about new ways to handle conflict?" Karoline asked the group.

"I would ask the person why they were mad at me and try to get them to talk about it."

"You could just play off the other person's stupid remarks instead of getting mad at them."

"I would go and get a teacher and ask her to handle the situation when it started to get wild."

"If you don't go off on another person, you don't become part of the problem. By refusing to be negative with them, you can try to find a solution and create peace. It is important that we try to love others as Jesus did," Karoline concluded.

As I watched her interaction with the group, I knew why Karoline had been volunteering with Young Friends the past four years. She had found a way to use her gifts in ministry.

Another college student who was active in ministry with the Fellowship of Friends was Linda. Linda had grown up in Cabrini as the oldest girl in a family of eight children. Highly motivated, she was an honor role student in high school, a participant in several sports, and an active member of the Fellowship of Friends. When Lisa Johanon moved to Detroit to began a new urban ministry in Youth for Christ, Linda took Lisa's position as Young Friends Coordinator. Her leadership skills were soon evident to all.

"Are you ready to go visiting today?" Linda said as she opened the door to the office.

I looked up from the typewriter where I had been finishing my remaining correspondence for the week. "Sure, let me finish this letter, and I'll be right with you."

Minutes later we walked out the door of the meetinghouse towards our first destination, 500 W. Oak, the red brick, nineteen-story highrise across the street.

As we approached the building, we passed a group of teenagers leaning against the entrance of their building marked with five-point stars graffiti.

"What's happenin'?" they said as we passed.

"How you doing?" we replied.

They were the familiar sentries for the building. Once in the darkened hallway we noticed one of the mothers checking her mailbox. A grocery cart filled with laundry stood next to her.

"Are the elevators working today?" Linda asked.

"At least for now," she smiled in response.

The elevator door slowly opened, and I said a silent prayer as we stepped inside. Public housing elevators were notorious for their breakdowns. My private dread was that we might be one of their next victims.

"Press eight. Let's visit Karen's mother to see if she can go to camp this summer," Linda suggested.

I breathed a sigh of relief when the doors opened without incident on the eighth floor. We turned to the right and walked to the end of the hallway and found Karen's apartment. Linda knocked on their screen door.

"Hi! Come on in," Karen's mother said as she opened the door with a smile.

I enjoyed visiting this family. Their apartment always seemed to have a warm cozy feeling.

"How is your mother doing, Linda?"

"Oh, she's just fine."

"I sure like all the pictures you have in your apartment," Linda commented as she glanced at the photographs which filled the walls of their living room.

"Yes, they're all pictures of our family. Here's one of Karen when she was younger," her mother said proudly as she handed us a photograph from the top of the of the television.

"Karen sure looks cute. I love her long French braids," I complimented.

"Come on in and sit down."

"Lavonna, we're here to ask you if Karen can go to camp with us this summer," Linda explained. "We are taking a group of twelve kids to a farm in Iowa, and we would like Karen to go. We are planning a boat ride on the Mississippi River, picnics, hay rides, and a visit to a dairy. Since they will be staying with a farm family, they will also be able to see all kinds of animals. Last year they were able to ride a horse. We will be gone two days. If Karen can go, the cost is $2 to reserve her a spot and $3 when she goes. What do you think?"

"It sounds great. In fact, can you take Alice? Although she is only five, she is mature for her age."

"Sure, if she promises to be good," Linda said with a smile.

"Why don't you sign them up, and I will come to the office

next week with the money," Karen's mother said.

"Thanks for letting them be a part of the Fellowship of Friends," we said as we walked out the door.

It was easy to get kids to go to camp. The Fellowship of Friends had gained a good reputation for the excellent camping program we offered each summer.

When the door had closed, Linda shared how she had known Karen's family when she was a young girl. Linda's family had lived in 500 W. Oak until they moved to 1230 N. Burling to get a bigger apartment. She still knew several of the families who lived in the building.

Once outside of the building, we noticed a group of boys pitching softball to each other. Standing in the outfield trying to catch a fly ball was one of the boys who had missed Young Friends the week before.

"Just a second, Marlene," Linda said as she walked up to him.

"Gerald, we missed you at Young Friends last week."

"I was at home," he replied.

"I sure hope you come back this week."

"Yeah, I'll be there," he said with a sheepish grin.

"I'll see you on Thursday," Linda responded.

We also took the opportunity to greet Gerald's cousins who were jumping rope nearby. They, too, were active in Young Friends.

"Why don't we stop by to let Altamease's and Gloria's mother know we missed her at church Sunday," I suggested as we crossed the field which separated 500 W. Oak from 1015 N. Larrabee.

As we walked passed the children on the swings, I thought how Linda had blossomed as a leader for Young Friends. Like so many other members, she had started as a participant in our high school program. Her love of the Lord made her one of the most committed members at worship and Bible studies. When she began working with Young Friends, her enjoyment of teaching the children was readily evident. Since she was studying accounting at college, I later trained her to also manage the finances of the Fellowship of Friends. She had

become an important role model for the children in the community. I wondered how we could encourage others to step out as
leaders, too.

During the following year we planned a self-evaluation of the
Fellowship of Friends which included problem solving and
goal setting. Numerous people in the community and program
were interviewed for their opinions. As a climax, we had a
retreat with a small group of leaders. After brainstorming
needs, we divided everyone into small groups to work on the
development of goals in each area of need. One of the primary
focus points was upon leadership development.

"I would be willing to help plan a leadership retreat this fall
for people in the Fellowship of Friends," offered Joan. "I think
we need to discuss the business procedures of the Quakers.
Many people do not have experience as a group in making
decisions. I could compare parliamentary procedure to the
Friends emphasis of viewing business as worship. This would
also lead us into a discussion of consensus."

"I'd like some help knowing how to handle kids in Young
Friends who get on my nerves," Gloria added.

"Let's include a discussion on the stages of child development at the retreat," I suggested. "Maybe it would help the
volunteers for the Youthquake and Young Friends programs."

"Maybe we could have weekly meetings for the high school
members with a focus upon leadership development," Steve
said excitedly. "Topics should focus on several areas which
would help prepare them for the future like job development,
financial planning, conflict resolution, marriage/family, and
visiting potential colleges."

"I'd like to teach a series of sessions on how they can improve
their communication skills," Joan volunteered. "I've given
several workshops in this area."

"How about the adults?" Charlotte suggested, "The Fellowship of Friends always does things for the kids. We need more
adults."

"That's a great idea!" Joan agreed. "Monthly adult outings
and an annual retreat would attract additional adults. I would

even be willing to begin an adult Bible study in my home."

As our group continued to dialogue, our brainstorming chart quickly filled with ideas: expansion of fall volunteer orientation meetings, mandatory weekly volunteer meetings to dialogue about programs and children, spring volunteer appreciation during meeting for worship, and many other dreams. Each of us then made commitments to implement certain goals.

When the retreat was finished, Steve and I went back to our rooms to prepare for our departure. I checked under the beds and through the drawers to make sure we had not forgotten anything in the room. Steve closed the suitcases and placed them near the door. I could tell his mind was still focused on our session.

"This has been a real turning point for the Fellowship of Friends," Steve said as he reached out to put his arm around me.

"What do you mean?" I replied.

"'This retreat has encouraged more people in the church to take greater ownership of the ministry," Steve explained. "Even though it will be a long process, leadership will begin to arise from the Fellowship of Friends to effectively reach out to the needs of the community."

Serving
the Wider
Community

9

I was sent of God to stand a witness against all
violence, and the words of darkness; and to turn
people from darkness to light and to bring them
from the causes of war and fighting to the peace-
able Gospel."

George Fox

"The Fellowship of Friends needs to be more involved in the community."

The words of our retreat leader continued to ring in my mind. Even though the Fellowship of Friends attempted to minister to the wholistic needs of the individual, she was convinced we needed to more visibly address community issues. If the community continued to disintegrate around us, it couldn't help but affect us.

Our first step was to become a part of the community's efforts to provide a safe place for the children to play during the summers. If we monitored the playgrounds in the afternoons, various churches and agencies could reclaim the community. Our primary focus became the playground across the street from our meetinghouse.

At first sight our playground appears as normal as any other throughout the city. Inside a large wire fence are two swing sets, a slide, and climbing equipment. Although it is sometimes in need of repair or garbage removal, the real problem is not visible to the average visitor to Cabrini. Standing on opposite sides of the playground are two large red brick highrises, 500 W. Oak and 1015 N. Larrabee. Each one is claimed as turf by opposite gangs. During the summer when teens are out of school with little to do, it becomes common for the two gangs to agitate each other. The playground then becomes an urban battleground. During the summer of 1985, a young nine-year-old girl, Laketa Crosby, was killed in Cabrini by a stray bullet from a gang fight. She was downstairs in her building innocently jumping rope. Our efforts to create a safe place for children to play became intensified.

Members of the Fellowship of Friends began to regularly visit the playground for two hours in the afternoon to provide recreation for the children on their playground.

"Is everyone ready?"

"OK, here comes the ball, Teresa," Trayce said as she rolled the ball towards a young girl who stood ready to kick it on home plate.

"Look out!"

"She really kicked it this time!"

"Catch it, Eddie."

"I got it!" grinned Teresa's brother, Eddie as he threw the ball back to Trayce.

Trayce was not only a great kickball pitcher, but she wanted to teach the children from the two buildings that they could play together on the same playground. A Quaker originally from Philadelphia, Trayce had spent three years as a teacher in Belize. Afterward, she moved to Chicago to become an active member of the Fellowship of Friends and to teach adult literacy with CYCLE. Her innate gifts of counseling and teaching strengthened our outreach to the community.

"One out for Teresa's team," added Steve.

"Come on, Doneta. Get a homerun this time!" cheered Trayce.

As Doneta kicked the ball hard into left field, everyone's eyes focused on a group of teens gathering just a few yards from the playground.

"They're at it again."

"Now they're throwing bottles."

"I hope they stay over there."

Doneta ran safely to second base, and Trayce prepared for the next pitch.

"Let's go, Richard. Kick it to the fence," Trayce yelled.

Again everyone's eyes focused on the outfield. This time it was obvious that the background action was drawing nearer. A group of teens from the 500 building began to run towards the playground on their way to the 1015 building.

"We've gotta get 'em out of here, Steve," warned Trayce.

"You got it," said Steve.

"Go home!" yelled Trayce.

Within minutes the children had scattered to their respective buildings with no questions asked. Already that summer, gunfire from gangs had shot people in both of their buildings.

Steve and Trayce rushed to the meetinghouse to call the police and alert them to the situation. Watching from the windows, they saw the boys from 500 return to their building. Later a group of teens from 1015 ran across the playground towards 500 to retaliate. By the time the police arrived, the action was over. It had all happened so fast. We were thankful that none of the children had been hurt.

Individuals from the Fellowship of Friends continued the vigil for peace. Parents began to express their appreciation for our presence on the playground. A few began to join us. One hot afternoon we played with the kids in the water from an open fire hydrant. Even the teens from the two different gangs couldn't resist the opportunity to cool each other off in the water. Slowly we began to attract others to join our time of play.

Besides the playground monitoring, churches and agencies sponsored a variety of community events that year. Worship services were planned on the playgrounds which included choir selections, prayers, and devotionals. Once we organized a walk through the community on Good Friday.

"What are the stations of the cross?" Robert asked.

"It is a time of worship where you remember the events which happened on Good Friday when Jesus died," I replied.

"But why are we walking through the community to do it? People don't normally walk around like this," he continued.

"We are trying to make a public witness to remind everyone how Jesus suffered that we might have peace," I explained.

Our group from the Fellowship of Friends continued to walk down Larrabee Street on our way to Strangers Home Baptist Church. Within minutes we joined the members of other community churches and agencies.

"Who would like to carry the cross?" A Franciscan brother asked.

"I would like to!" volunteered Linda. "I want to walk with the cross by my building. She raised the cross to her shoulder and walked at the head of the group toward the 1230 N. Burling high rise.

"Were you there when they crucified my Lord?" our group members sang.

The singing and cross drew the attention of numerous by-standers who turned their heads to see our procession. Some of the children ran over eagerly to the group to join our walk briefly past their building.

When we reached her station, Linda read the appropriate liturgy, "The mother of Jesus was near him in his suffering and death. What sorrow and grief must have been borne in her breast — for she was like any mother who suffers when her children suffer. It is easy to imagine her running to Jesus as a boy to mend a skinned knee and kiss away his tears. Now she had to stand by and watch his pain, unable to stop the blood or soothe his brow."

We responded, "Good Father, forgive us for the pain our sins caused this poor mother. We pray, too, for the mothers in our community who suffer as they watch their sons and daughters.

Forgive us, too, Lord, for allowing them to suffer so long. Help those mothers and fathers whose children have suffered and died violent deaths — like the mother of your son, they too, have suffered much."

"Father, heal our community and let violence cease," Linda prayed.

"Amen," we said in unison.

Even though the Fellowship of Friends normally did not worship with liturgy, it seemed appropriate for that day as we joined with so many of our Christian brothers and sisters from a variety of denominational backgrounds. Just as Christ Jesus suffered violence unjustly and triumphed over it, so we could arise in unity to work for peace in Cabrini-Green.

The tragedy is that the coalition which began the playground monitoring has been laid down. Initially the community coalition included churches, agencies, and community residents. Although this diversity was our strength, it was also our weakness. The various participants brought their own agendas for the group's purpose and goals. This broad diversity in agendas created conflict and power struggles which several individuals were unwilling to resolve to find community unity. Although we could agree on what the problems were, we could not agree on the solutions.

In addition to community violence, our meeting was also concerned about the need for emergency shelter. At various times we had been requested to open our home to troubled teens by parents, community workers, or the young people themselves. The reasons for the refuge were varied — family violence, gang threats, or runaways. One young girl in particular moved our hearts.

"Marlene, I have to talk with you!" Trayce said with a frantic look on her face. "Can you give me a few minutes in the conference room?"

I followed Trayce into the small conference room at the meetinghouse and sat down on the sofa next to her.

"I have a big favor to ask of you. I really need your help, or I should say Almeta does. She needs a place to stay for a while.

As you know she has been staying from house to house since she had her baby. It just isn't working. Her grades are going down, and if it keeps up, she won't graduate," Trayce explained.

"Have you contacted the community agencies?" I asked.

"Yes, we have worked with several of them. Some of them have provided food or clothing, but there are just no housing options. The Department of Children and Family Services does not want to get involved because she is almost eighteen. The Chicago Housing Authority will not give her an apartment because she is not eighteen. It becomes a vicious circle, and she is slipping through their cracks," lamented Trayce.

"Let me talk to Steve, and we'll try to work out something," I tried to encourage her.

After talking with Steve, and later with Almeta, arrangements were made for her and her newborn baby to stay with us. I would hear Almeta get up at 6:00 a.m. to quickly dress, feed the baby, and leave to catch the bus for the baby sitter's home. From there she was off to an early morning class at the high school. Her extra effort brought her a coveted high school diploma in June. Soon she received word that she was accepted as a freshman at Northeastern University in Chicago. Her dreams had not died.

Almeta also was a great mother and made sure the baby's needs were always met. When Denise, her baby, caught a cold, she and her boyfriend made arrangements for medical help. She spent time loving her baby and playing with her.

With Trayce's encouragement, Almeta and her boyfriend received counseling about their relationship. Reconciliation also began with her parents. They began to save money to look for their own apartment.

She also became a regular attender at the Fellowship of Friends and joined the choir. At times I would find Almeta lying on her bed reading the Bible for encouragement. Almeta had needed a stable place to stay, a little encouragement, and a renewal of her faith in God.

Our concern for emergency shelter was also felt by another

member, Barb. Barb joined us as we began the Fellowship of Friends. After serving as a volunteer for several years, she decided to go back to graduate school to obtain a degree in social work. Her primary goal was to begin an emergency shelter for children in the Cabrini-Green area. However, the dream was not without frustration.

"Marlene, you really need to pray for me and the home," Barb said one day as she slipped into the chair next to my desk.

"How is it coming?" I asked.

"Sometimes it is so discouraging. So many groups don't want to give unless we have an established program. Yet, if we can't get the money, how can we get established? Other sources of funding are extremely political," she explained.

"I know what you mean about that. Yet, you have such a great board and program, someone is bound to provide the money," I sympathized.

"We are also having a difficult time finding space. People know there is a need, but communities don't want troubled teenagers living in their neighborhood," she added.

"I'd offer you space in the meetinghouse, but the Fellowship of Friends and CYCLE have already grown so fast we have problems scheduling the space for groups using it now. We need to pray the Lord will provide us with space and the finances to develop it," I encouraged.

The continuing need for housing has also led us to help young married couples and college students find housing outside of Cabrini. Chicago Housing Authority's regulations have prohibited college students from obtaining their own apartments in Cabrini unless they have children. Many of the junior colleges or major universities do not have sufficient housing for students. The Quaker Volunteer Witness apartment was our first venture in this area.

Originally the Quaker Volunteer Witness apartment was developed to provide housing for young people who wished to volunteer a year of their lives with the Fellowship of Friends. Our first volunteers were Loren and Debbie Boettcher from Friends Bible College. The second year, Brian Young, a

Quaker college student from Maryland, became a part of QVW as well as two young adults, Charlie and Lonzo, from the Fellowship of Friends. Charlie worked full-time at a grocery store but needed an apartment on the West Side close to his job. Lonzo worked full-time at a contact lens manufacturing firm and went to college part-time. Chicago Housing Authority wanted to take 30 percent of his paycheck if he remained in Cabrini with his mother and family. Alone, these young men could not afford an apartment, but together they could.

We have also helped people who needed to find a job, seek legal assistance, or gain entrance into college. Our ministry has sought to meet the wide variety of needs in the individual's life. In addition to being available to those in need, a primary goal is continuing to teach the children of the next generation that there is hope for their lives and the community.

"We have been talking about how being a Christian can bring peace to our individual lives in Junior High Young Friends. Tonight we have two guest speakers from the police department who want to talk to us about how we can work together to bring peace to the community," I began. "This is our beat representative and an officer from the police department. I want you to listen closely to what they have to say."

The police officer walked to the front of the group. Even though he was dressed in his uniform, his smile and warmth helped to put the children at ease.

"Tonight I want to talk with you about youth and the law. Many times young people do not realize that listening to other people who suggest that they do something that is wrong can get them into serious trouble," the officer warned.

"By trying to please them you can be arrested and sent to prison. These people are often only using you to do what would get them in trouble. If you hold their guns, steal for them, or sell their drugs they feel your punishment in Juvenile Court will be less severe. However, why should you sacrifice your future just to please them and endanger yourselves by illegal acts?" he continued.

For the next twenty minutes the young people listened

closely to the officer. Then came a time of discussion.

"I got in trouble once and had to go wash graffiti off of the CTA buses."

"The people in my building are always after me to do drugs with them."

"You just have to say 'no' when they want you to do bad stuff."

As the meeting came to a close, the officer stood at the door in preparation to continue the discussion with the high school teens.

"I have something I want to give you," one of the junior high kids said softly.

"Sure, what is it?" asked the officer.

"I don't think I should hold these anymore," the young boy said as he held out a handful of bullets.

I looked in shock at the ammunition he was carrying. Then I remembered his brother was a gang member. No doubt the evening's discussion had prompted him to think about issues which affected him closely.

"I'd be glad to take these, young man! Thank you!" the officer said with a smile.

I gave the boy a hug. Yes, there was hope for the future.

What Can
Friends Offer
the City?

10

---

*"If there be any kindness I can show, or any
good thing I can do, let me do it now, let me not
deter or neglect it, for I shall not pass this way
again."*

Stephen Grellet

"Today we are going to learn the secret of church growth,"
the speaker confidently informed us. He began a series of
overhead projections of statistical graphs to prove his point.

The yearly meeting had invited a church growth expert to do
a workshop on expansion strategies for the Society of Friends.
We sat with notebooks ready to jot down the key ingredients
which would enliven our meetings.

"One of the first principles is that churches which are
homogeneous are the ones which grow," the expert continued.
"People like to worship with those who are like them."

"Oh, no," I whispered to Steve. The speaker's words pierced
my ears like a knife. I guessed what his next words were going
to be.

"You need to survey the potential communities where a

church could be planted to discover if they would respond to your market. Decide who you want to reach and target your minister, location and publicity to attract the target group."

As the church growth expert continued, I cringed in my chair. If we took this seriously, we would target white, middle-upperclass, well-educated neighborhoods to continue a homogeneous concept of church. If these technigrowth experts were followed, we would neglect the poor and diverse urban communities of our country.

This model has been followed by some Quakers. Instead of a commitment to explore new avenues for ministry, Friends have been afraid to face the unknown. Just last year we learned of several Friends meetings in poor, urban communities which have been "laid down." Friends meetinghouses in Seattle, Washington; San Diego, California; Birmingham, England; and Dayton, Ohio, have been sold to other denominations. Some meetings have fled poor communities to new buildings in wealthier areas. This scenario is not unique to the Society of Friends; it has been repeated in several Protestant denominations.

Another current model for urban ministry is to enter a neighborhood to assist and then "spin off" the ministry to become independent at the first opportunity. Numerous social service agencies, for instance, have roots in a church or denomination and developed from this approach. Quakers also have started many worthy projects and institutions which later bear no witness to our name or theology. Why do we not share our theology and invite others to join us? Why do we restrict so many from decision-making for the future of Quakers? Are we afraid of becoming personally involved in ministry?

Throughout our history, Friends have not only advocated social change, but invested their personal lives and finances in the causes in which they believed. In the earliest days of Quakerism, Swarthmoor Hall was a financial center for traveling ministers. Margaret Fell and her family kept faithful accounts of disbursements ranging from finances to clothing which enabled Quaker ministers to take their message throughout England. Their commitment to administrate this effort led to the rapid expansion of early Friends. In the United States, Levi Coffin became known as the Father of the Underground Railroad not merely because he was an armchair abolitionist, but because he personally transported countless individuals as they escaped slavery to freedom. Susan B. Anthony and Lucretia Mott were not cloistered in their Friends meetings when they provided leadership for the women's suffrage movement. Their political rallies are legendary. Jane Addams did not remain in her comfortable Quaker home in rural Illinois to begin her innovative settlement houses for immigrants throughout Chicago. Her ministry was an outgrowth of personal commitment to the needs she witnessed. Where is this Quaker legacy of active personal ministry in response to convictions in our present Friends meetings?

How can we honestly maintain a testimony of equality for all if we run from opportunities to minister among people who are different from "us?" The Religious Society of Friends began during a time when people were dissatisfied with the hypocrisy which existed in the organized church. George Fox believed that faith must honestly be lived out daily. In fact, the early Friends received such a reputation for integrity in their convictions and honesty in business that numerous products were named after them. Will we respond to opportunities to live out our testimony of equality in urban areas and among the poor and someday become a model for others in the areas of church growth? Or will we follow the current models and lay down our testimony of equality? Are we willing to live the faith we profess?

As is true with many older Protestant denominations which have outlived numerous trends in the religious world, the whole message of the Gospel of Christ Jesus has been divided within the Religious Society of Friends. A liberal faction emphasizes doing above believing. Members are known for lobbying efforts in countless worthy causes—nuclear disarmament, justice in Central America, protection of the environment, and ending apartheid in South Africa. However, little unity exists in theological areas, and countless young people leave their meetings because they sense a spiritual vacuum. Quaker fundamentalists, on the other hand, hold a strong Christology, but often lack a commitment to the intense discipleship which led to the historical Quaker testimonies. These are the extremes which a weary Quaker middle tries to bring together. Out of these ashes of division and strife needs to arise the rebirth of the *whole* message of Quakerism. We need to affirm that Christ Jesus is the answer to our spiritual hunger and that the reality of the indwelling spirit leads us to forsake the ways of the world and live distinctively from the sin and evil which surround us.

It is this *whole* message of Quakerism which waits to be told in urban areas today. The poor need to hear that Christ loves them regardless of their material possessions, and that simplicity of lifestyle frees them to follow Christ more completely. Victims of prejudice need to hear that the seed of God dwells in all, waiting to grow in the light of Christ Jesus and bring them into the true church of Christ Jesus which sees beyond human divisions. The oppressed need to know that they, too, have gifts of ministry which should be developed so that they can confront the oppressor and their injustice. Those caught in substance abuse need to hear the message that the indwelling power of Christ can free them from the pain and insanity they have experienced. The alienated and alone need to experience the sense of community and love which comes from knowing the eternal Friend and becoming a part of Christ's followers. Our message can no longer afford to be divided.

The Chicago Fellowship of Friends strives to teach and model the Quaker message which is so relevant to the needs existing in urban areas. In contrast to the homogeneous church growth model, we emphasize the Quaker principle that there is a seed of God in all people and through Christ Jesus all are equal (Ephesians 2:11-22; Colossians 3:11). Members of our meeting come from diverse backgrounds of class and culture. While some urban ministries strive to recruit only the leaders of the community for their programs, we are willing to work closely with the teens who are often a part of the Juvenile Court system. These young people often take more effort and tough love; yet God loves even them (Matthew 25:31-46). The Quaker belief that women, too, are equally called into ministry helps to affirm the dignity and worth of those women who suffer from the pain of poverty in urban areas.

Our belief that we are not the only ones predestined with God's ministry allows us the freedom to network with other urban groups. C.U.R.E. (Chicago Urban Reconciliation Enterprise) allows our young people opportunities to regularly worship and fellowship with other churches in the Chicago area. We actively participate in a Swedish Covenant Basketball League and are considered a mission project of the Oakdale Swedish Covenant Church. We also receive funding from other Chicagoland churches. We have provided urban ministry training for students from Moody Bible Institute, McCormick Theological Seminary, Bethany Seminary, and Northern Baptist Seminary. We continue to participate with other churches for special community events.

Since God loves all individuals and equips the members of the church with special spiritual gifts, the Chicago Fellowship of Friends emphasizes the empowerment of individuals in the meeting for ministry and community formation (Ephesians 4:1-16). Our members are encouraged to serve as volunteers in the ministry with younger children and community work projects. We choose to develop indigenous leadership rather than to always bring in leadership from the outside. We challenge our young people to "reach back" in ministry and return to the community as they grow older. This emphasis on volunteerism is often in contrast to a model which stresses professional care-giving programs. The belief in the priesthood of the believer and the empowerment of all in the meeting for ministry is primary to Quakerism. In the early 1800s a Quaker, Joseph Lancaster, took this Quaker theological principle and applied it to education by enlisting older students to teach younger children under the supervision of a trained master. This concept of empowerment needs to be reapplied to urban ministry today.

The Quaker principle of honesty is also relevant in urban ministry. In a setting where words are often meaningless, the integrity of religious belief and lifestyle is appealing. Often the church has failed to communicate its message because it has relied on impersonal words or tracts. When people have suffered injustice and poverty, more than words is needed. The church needs to "earn the right to be heard" through its actions.

It took nine difficult months of groundwork by Steve before we got our first formal group together. Since we began our work in the winter, the streets were fairly empty. Steve began by setting up basketball games with a core group of eight or nine boys who had responded to earlier ministries in the area. A few girls I met at the games also became regulars in the group.

We drew our first ten summer campers from that group the following season. Even that summer, Steve remembers feeling intimidated by the culture he found on the playground.

"I was very conscious of being white," he says, "and I was fearful because of all the rumors I'd heard about violence. I also didn't play ball very well then, and I didn't know the customs of the playground or how to pick up teams. I made a lot of mistakes and would leave the playground feeling like a fool.

"What I learned was that playground action is like a courtroom. The arguments and yelling are, in fact, just the way they work. Where I came from, when there was yelling and arguing it was a prelude to a fight. Here it is just part of the game, and the one who argues in the most logical manner wins. In fact, if the arguing on these playgrounds leads to fighting it is a sign of weakness.

"I had a lot to learn. In those early days, most of the work was very informal—a Coke after a game, a trip to Great America. It *is* intimidating to enter any other culture. Hanging in there is the most important thing."

Steve's ministry through setting up basketball teams for the community still draws young people to the message they see lived out in the lives of Steve and other Fellowship of Friends members of the team. Often those kids who are new to the program begin to attend meeting for worship seeking the answers to why we are different. Honestly living out our faith and telling others our Good News is what draws people into the kingdom of God.

Simplicity is also attractive to many who suffer in poverty. Many churches stress dressing up to attend their worship. It is refreshing to find a church which emphasizes not the outward appearance, but what is happening within one's spiritual life. While many churches concern themselves with maintenance of elaborate physical plants, the simplicity seen in many Friends meetinghouses allows for more finances to be spent in ministry. The emphasis on elaborate written rituals or creeds is not found in Quaker meetings where the central issue is remaining faithful to the Lord's calling within each individual's life. This message is often unheard.

Finally, the testimony of peace and justice holds great appeal for those suffering from violence and poverty. Once people find inner peace with God, they can respond in love to those around them and seek just solutions to conflicts. The commitment of individuals to seek justice leads to peace within the larger community. In urban areas which are often torn with selfish hatred, injustice, and violence, this message can be healing balm to those who suffer.

The Fellowship of Friends strives to model this Quaker theology in an urban context. Unifying the whole message of Quakerism within our ministry has meant we have received support from across the various divisions of Quakerism. We have also provided leadership training for young people who are interested in urban ministry. As we have traveled in the ministry we have created an awareness among Quakers for the need to minister in urban areas. We hope to provide greater opportunities for communication, unity, and ministry within the Religious Society of Friends.

This ministry to the Religious Society of Friends can be

reciprocal. Through stewardship of resources from Friends meetings which have financial security, we can not only increase the ministry of the Fellowship of Friends, but train others who dream of responding to the need of urban ministry in other communities. Friends can commit to praying for our needs as we daily face conflict with sin and evil. Meetings can challenge members to embrace those in their communities who may be suffering from poverty or injustice. Together we can unite in ministry to meet the needs around us.

Will the Religious Society of Friends unite to take its message to urban communities in need? Can we reach out to others who may be different from "us," or will our focus continue to be upon our own preservation? Are we willing to move beyond our historic Quaker laurels to minister creatively for Christ Jesus today? Are Quakers willing to be good stewards of their personal gifts of ministry, financial resources, and time to make urban ministry effective?

Lessons From the City

11

"Why should we so much try to keep something back, and not be willing to offer ourselves up to Him, body, soul, and spirit, to do with us what may seem best unto Him, and to make us what He would have us to be? O Lord! enable me to be more and more, singly, simply, and purely obedient to Thy service!"

Elizabeth Fry

A frequent question of many concerned with the needs of the urban poor is how to implement an effective strategy for ministry. From our pilgrimage as the Fellowship of Friends, we have learned the importance of several key components.

1. Identify Your Personal Style of Ministry and Gifts. Each believer possesses certain talents and resources which are a blessing from our Creator to be used to serve those around us and build God's Kingdom. We all have something to give, and our ministries are unique. The church provides an avenue for our various gifts to join together to strengthen one another's witness. Rather than lay persons feeling they must duplicate a

85

"professional minister's role," they should feel the liberation and support to identify strengths and weaknesses and use them wisely as God's stewards.

Once we have evaluated our style of ministry and gifts, we are often called to "bloom where we are planted." If you are living in a large metropolitan area, your primary focus might be the needs on your doorstep. Seek out a church in your community which is concerned with meeting the needs of the urban poor. If you are already attending a church, seek ways to strengthen its mission to its immediate community. If you are living in a community where the needs are going unmet by the church, begin to pray about taking the initiative to use your gifts to meet them.

2. Research the Community. Before you begin any program or buy a building, take time to do your homework on the needs of the community. If statistics are available from other groups, get them. Otherwise gather your own data. Read about the history of the area. This often explains why and how the community has its needs. Survey residents to gather current information. Take time to meet with community leaders (police, educators, politicians, business leaders) for their reflections on the community. Articulate your concerns as well.

Assess what churches currently exist in the area. Are their constituents primarily from the community, or do they drive into it on Sundays? Have the churches undergone a community transition which has left them depleted and yearning for a former constituency? Are there any signs of active community concerns and outreach?

If the community is filled with active churches ministering to the needs of the majority of the residents, duplication of services would be an unwise use of resources. If not, it might be a sign for an open door.

3. Seek Clearness and Prayer. Once you have identified the needs of the community, share your vision of ministry with other Christians who know you well. Ask them to pray with you for clearness as you seek to reach out to meet the needs you have identified. Often they will be able to provide insight and

guidance which might otherwise go unnoticed. They may even challenge your weaknesses. Most importantly, they will join you in seeking to have your leading confirmed.

After you have received clearness as to your leading in ministry, call the church to prayer. Ask them to pray with you for every aspect of the ministry you will face. Whenever a Christian attempts to reach out into areas of need and oppression, there is conflict with the evil which has caused the needs. Without prayer support and spiritual maturity, it is easy to crumble when faced with such evil. However, the support of the church through prayer and love will provide strength to persevere through even the most difficult moments. Without this support, it is easy to burn out.

4. Share Your Vision. Once your leading is confirmed, begin to share your vision of ministry with others. Attempt to provide a bridge for needed resources in the community and ministry.

Ministry in poor urban areas often calls for fundraising from other sources beyond the resources of the community which is served. Attend fundraising seminars to learn how to write proposals and develop a financial base. Get acquainted with the corporate foundations and trusts in your metropolitan area. Develop a newsletter which will communicate your activities and dreams. Accept speaking engagements at other churches and extend to them an invitation to support your ministry. Develop a strategy for public relations.

It is also important to organize and develop human resources. Many urban ministries operate with a board which is primarily composed of people from outside the community who offer their skills and resources to the organization. At times there may be a community advisory board which assists this primary board. If a ministry develops through an existing church, the present board and a committee focused on the developing ministry may be adequate organizational support. The church will need to decide if the ministry should be incorporated independently and raise their finances separately, or if the church is willing to assume the primary care of the ministry.

Lines of authority and decision-making need to be clearly set.

It is also important to learn what city-wide resources currently exist which can receive referrals from your community. In effective ministry there needs to be a focus upon the wholistic development of each person. Develop contacts with those resource areas which can provide assistance in a variety of areas: justice, health, education, financial, political, and employment.

5. Set Purpose and Goals. Gather together the core group of people who have responded to your vision of ministry in the community and together develop your purpose statement and related goals to accomplish your purpose. Spend time brainstorming about the needs in the community and avenues to meet them. Once your purpose has been established, this will provide a distinct identity for your ministry. The goals will give you an initial focus, but will need to be continually evaluated and refocused.

The goals for the ministry will reflect the programs for ministry. Research other models of ministry in this area and gain ideas from their program development, curriculum or training. If your focus is upon young single mothers, learn about what type of counseling guidelines have been developed for them. If your focus is junior high ministry, investigate the numerous resources available in youth ministry. If your focus is upon housing, read all the available materials which exist from others who have ventured into this area of need.

This foundation of ministry focus leads to the development of a budget and other resources to support the ministry. Creatively seek funding from a variety of sources — individual pledges, foundations, fundraisers, mail appeals, and the support of the church. Rather than buying an expensive building, you may wish to rent space, use your church's facilities, or renovate an older structure.

6. Develop Leadership. You will need staff and/or volunteers to carry out programs. Often when a ministry begins, there is a limited budget for staff salaries. It is vital to enlist the support of others. Volunteer training not only allows others to use their gifts of ministry, but expands your capacity for ministry. Recruit individuals who identify with your purpose, and then develop a training manual for their use. Some groups prefer retreats for their time of training; others plan weekly seminars. Develop volunteer job descriptions. Once volunteers have begun their ministry, plan regular volunteer staff meetings to discuss their feedback, answer questions, share resource ideas, and plan together. Include times when you can show your appreciation for your volunteers and their dedication.

A temptation of many larger organizations who decide to begin a ministry in a poor urban community is to bring all their leadership from outside of the community. Although it takes longer to train leadership from within the community, efforts should be made to empower individuals to develop their gifts of ministry. Take time to train people within the community how to operate in committees, develop programs, monitor finances, handle conflict, and work together. The result will not only be a more successful program, but leadership and community development as well.

7. Focus on the Individual. Effective program development and its administration can never replace one of the key components of an effective urban ministry, incarnation of the love and message of Christ to individuals.

This critical component is a unique contribution which the church can make to the community. Many service organizations focus upon programs rather than individuals. Once the program is over or their one area of service is completed, the individual is forgotten. The church can affirm the importance of each individual in God's sight.

Through wholistic care and ministry to the individual, Christ's love becomes a reality for their lives. You may often spend ninety percent of your ministry time being with people and meeting their needs to earn the right to be heard. Through your commitment to develop a relationship with the individual, the message of Christ becomes alive and meaningful. Mere words do not speak as strongly as a life which has been transformed by the power of God.

Effective evangelism must always be coupled with discipleship. Ministry should include a deliberate commitment to provide a support group which will nurture individuals through their struggles and to provide a sense of community. Care giving can become personalized to each individual as the church seeks ways to enable people to become all God created them to be.

8. Commit Yourself. When we first began working in Cabrini-Green, I knew we would go through a time of testing which teenagers often give to adults. However, I never anticipated one question which I repeatedly was asked, "How long will you be here?" These young people wondered if they could really trust us to be there for them.

In a community in which programs come and go according to changes in government funding and trends, young people learn to build defenses to keep adult leaders from getting too close. It hurts to let someone become close and then have them leave abruptly. The urban church needs to affirm the traditional model of the parish priest who commits his life and time to care for those who are within the boundaries of the community.

9. Remain Centered. In the midst of urban poverty and pain it is easy to fall into the "messiah" complex where you feel compelled to rush to each emergency which calls. It is easy to become so divided by worthy causes that you are often ineffective in any area of ministry. Stewardship of ourselves in the areas of diet, rest, exercise, and emotional support is also a priority in ministry. An awareness should exist of personal limitations and needs in these areas. Time must be made daily, weekly and annually to set priorities. Once priorities are set, do the hard work of learning how to say "no."

Active ministry necessitates times of renewal. Through regular periods of silence, prayer and devotions, one is able to not merely go through the motions of ministry but to portray the spirit of Christ Jesus throughout the day. New insight and guidance for ministry are often the result of reflection and prayer. It also is important to have a time of prayer with others who are committed in ministry with you. The Quaker tradition of silent worship in the gathered community of faith becomes a powerful time of renewal for corporate ministry.

It is also important to schedule a time of sabbatical every few years. This should be an extended period of several months set aside for renewal outside the community through rest, play, prayer and study. Your support group should be responsible for seeing that you care for yourself in this way.

10. Dare to Confront Sin and Evil. Human need is often caused by selfishness and injustice. The urban church must renew its voice as a prophet to speak against the individual sins and corporate evils which face our society.

Early Quakers spent much time in jail and in the stocks as they attempted to confront the injustices that surrounded them. Their adoption of the peace testimony came out of their personal suffering against evil and their abhorrence of violence in any form. They took courage in the witness of Christ who willingly accepted the cross as His witness of love.

Today's church must continue to be active in applying the message of Christ to its community. Individuals who are struggling in personal sins need to be confronted. Corrupt institutions need to be held accountable. The church cannot afford to live an isolated "cocoon" existence from the world. The Spirit of Christ can provide us with the wisdom, love and patience needed to confront the evil on our doorstep.

These ten aspects of effective ministry can strengthen the church's witness in our cities today. Are we open to liberate others to reach out in new ways of ministry? Are we committed to bridge the necessary resources to empower those in need? Are we willing to take the role of priest and prophet in our urban areas today?

Theology of
Urban Ministry

12

"To labor for a perfect redemption from this spirit of oppression is the great business of the whole family of Christ Jesus in this world."
John Woolman

The growing gap in the United States between the wealthy and the poor is increasingly evident to many today. Even after the government's War Against Poverty, we have allowed a culture of permanent poverty to take root in our cities. A vicious cycle of illiteracy, unemployment, drug abuse, crime, violence, broken families, loneliness and pain have trapped many lives. Urban poverty can no longer be ignored. What theology of urban ministry can the church offer?

1. Message of Hope in Pain. Feelings of despair, apathy, self-centeredness, and disillusionment can be conquered with a vision of hope for the future. Drug abuse has become epidemic as people try individually to escape the pain. Some build their private nest with material possessions and pleasures to isolate their lives from the outside world. When they can no longer escape their pain and depression, some people erupt in open violence, while others turn the violence upon themselves in suicide. The inward soul seeks answers from a multitude of "earthly idols," but the real answers come from yielding to their heavenly Creator and allowing the Lord to shape their lives.

The message of Christ must continue to be told to those whose lives are in need of hope. They can personally experience God and divine, life-changing power. Confession of individual failure, the gift of forgiveness, the affirmation of life, and the sense of purpose for life continue to be an ageless salve to bring inner healing and positive growth. The assurance that God can be their eternal Friend must be given. Each person has a variety of needs in his or her life. The modern tragedy is that the spiritual component often has been overlooked. It is genuinely finding the center of one's life in God, however, which brings the remainder of one's life into divine harmony.

The church has struggled to effectively communicate this hope in Christ Jesus. The Protestant Reformation brought with it the division of the church, and in this country, the separation of many denominations across racial and class lines. Often we choose to worship with those who are like us and exclude those who are different. This commitment to homogeneous church growth has left certain groups in this country untouched with the Gospel.

The early church struggled with this, too. In the tenth chapter of Acts, Peter received a vision from God of a sheet which contained unclean animals being let down to earth. He heard a voice from heaven which asked him to arise and eat. After the vision occurred three times (a special number for Peter), Peter heard a knock at the door. Before him stood three men with the request that Peter come to the home of a Roman centurion, Cornelius. Within Jewish tradition Peter would have become unclean by entering Cornelius' home. However, Peter now understood the significance of the vision. He followed the men to minister to Cornelius and his household. "I now realize how true it is that God does not show favoritism but accepts men from every nation who fear him and do what is right" (Acts 10:34, 35).

Shortly thereafter, the account is given of the church of Antioch where the believers were first called Christians. This church grasped the concept of unity in Christ Jesus. Their leadership cut across lines of race and class: Barnabas (a mainline Jew from Jerusalem), Simeon (called Niger, Latin for black, probably of dark complexion), Lucius (from Northern Africa, Cyrene), Manean (from the upper class since he was the foster brother of Herod), and Paul (zealous Pharisee and ex-persecutor of Christians). It was this church of great diversity, but unified in Christ which sent Paul and Barnabas on their first missionary journey with the message of hope in Christ Jesus.

In today's urban centers many people have entertained the illusion that "they" are the saviors, and they enter a community with preconceived plans and programs. Often unaware that their cultural background clouds their mission, these people wonder why the community does not embrace their offers for help. They soon become disillusioned and leave.

Although one can come into a community with a preconceived purpose and message, the implementation of effective ministry can only be gained by respecting the people to whom one ministers and by listening to their needs. Token Thanksgiving baskets and used clothing may not be the real needs the community would identify for the church to meet. People need to hear the message of hope effectively applied to their real needs.

This has been difficult for some who minister in the city. One afternoon our basketball team was waiting for a ride to a game at a church which was sponsoring a workshop on evangelism. It was lunch time, and the workshop participants had stopped to enjoy chicken dinners. Obviously tempted at the smell of chicken, one of our teens walked into the room to see what was happening. Quickly someone shared the gospel principles in a tract with him and offered him something to eat. Without hesitation, he returned to his friends with the announcement that there was free food for them, too, if they were willing to say "yes" to becoming a Christian. Soon they all emerged from the room joking about how they had got their free chicken.

Is there a more effective approach to sharing the life-changing message of Christ then incorporating our society's surface-marketing techniques?

2. Authentic Life of the Messenger. Our society today has few genuine heroes for children. By emphasis on the best "outward package," many have fallen far when their "inward package" became exposed. Our media is filled with stories of politicians, movie stars, TV evangelists, and corporate businesspeople who outwardly portrayed an image of success and power but hid corruption, immorality, greed and oppression. Words have become cheap and not easily trusted. Thus, the message of the church cannot simply be left to the spoken or printed word. The message of Christ must be incarnated through the lives of obedient Christians in areas where hope is needed.

People have become disillusioned with the mixed message of many Christians and churches. A salvation which is experienced but which does not change a person's life often becomes a rationale for non-Christians to scoff at the church's ineffectiveness. As young people in Cabrini-Green would say, "We are tired of Christians who do not 'walk their talk.' " What is the point of joining a church which appears more like a club than a church? If it doesn't really make a difference, why not join the health club, a bowling team, or any other social club? The message of a hypocrite falls upon deaf ears.

The messenger of the church must be authentic. Christ warned the disciples to be cautious of false prophets who appear as wolves in sheep's clothing. "Not everyone who says to me, 'Lord, Lord,' will enter the kingdom of heaven, but only he who does the will of my Father who is in heaven. Many will say to me on that day, 'Lord, Lord, did we not prophesy in your name, and in your name drive out demons and perform many miracles?' Then I will tell them plainly, 'I never knew you. Away from me, you evildoers' " (Matthew 7:21-23).

We must develop a theology of the cross. Dietrich Bonhoeffer, the famous twentieth-century martyr who lived during Hitler's oppression, warned the church to beware of "cheap grace." Shallow Christianity, however, continues to pervade our society which has made faith comfortable and easy to live. For many, faith becomes mental acknowledgment of certain creedal beliefs which have little to do with their daily lifestyles. God becomes a "Santa Claus" figure to whom we simply pray for everything from a new car to financial wealth. If one suffers, he or she is doing something wrong. Although we *do* suffer when we face the consequences of our sin, suffering can also result from a life committed to obediently living the Gospel of Christ Jesus in an evil world. One must only look at the lives of prophets or to Jesus himself to see this reality.

The authentic Christian life is a life deeply committed to communicating Christ, even when the dream stage has ended and the reality of "sin" and "evil" face us. Stress and suffering have a way of bringing out hidden weaknesses which may be extremely uncomfortable; we may even try to deny or rationalize that these feelings exist. However, to effectively communicate the message of Christ, we must obediently face our own "crosses" and experience our individual resurrection which stems from such pain. When facing hardcore evil, we can become "burned out" or disillusioned if the message has not become a reality for our individual lives.

Educators have long known the importance of positive role models. If parents tell their children not to indulge in certain negative behavior and yet continue to accept it as right for themselves, then what they actually do with their lives will have a stronger impact than what they say. The same is true of the church. Do we continually evaluate our individual and corporate lives as to how authentically we are living the message of Christ Jesus? Have we been infiltrated by the pervasive philosophies propagated in our materialistic, self-centered society?

3. Committed Ministry of Servanthood. Many urban areas have become places of tremendous power and power struggles. Emphasis is placed on who you know. People strive to build relationships with the "right" people, and relationships become tools of manipulation to further careers or selfish motives. The ultimate goal is to take care of oneself.

Often the urban dweller's ideal is to live in the "right" neighborhood and only drive through the areas of need or read about them in the paper. To ease the sense of guilt for those less fortunate, people contribute financially to impersonal telethons, mail appeals, or pleas at the office. Many communities have turned care-giving over to institutions for those who are handicapped, elderly, poor, or criminals.

Many churches have also adopted this attitude about caring. Ministry to those in need has become professionalized; it is something someone else is paid to do. While any contribution is better than none, the major significance is to become personally involved in caring and serving others.

The New Testament Church embraced the ministry of servanthood for the poor. When Paul went before the Jerusalem Church to explain his ministry to the Gentiles, this message was affirmed. The church leaders consented to the freedom of the new Gentile believers who were not adhering to the Jewish law of circumcision. The pillars of the Jerusalem Church who were Christ's disciples (James, Peter and John) gave Paul the hand of fellowship and affirmed his ministry. The one condition they gave him was that his followers must continue to remember the poor (Galatians 2:1-10).

The importance of this teaching can also be seen in the writings of these three disciples. It is James who wrote the early church and condemned their favoritism for the wealthy and their neglect of the poor (James 2:5-6). He finished the chapter by warning the church that faith without works is dead.

Peter, too, wrote in his first epistle that our faith is greater than gold (I Peter 1:18). The one woman whom Peter raised from the dead was Dorcas (Acts 9:36-42). Dorcas was the early disciple who was known for her good works and all that she did for the poor.

Finally, John charged the early Christians to love one another and to give to those in need. "This is how we know what love is: Jesus Christ laid down his life for us. And we ought to lay down our lives for our brothers. If anyone has material possessions and sees his brother in need but has no pity on him, how can the love of God be in him? Dear children, let us not love with words or tongue but with actions and in truth" (1 John 3:16-18).

The difficult ministry of servanthood means effectively caring for the needs of people and more importantly modeling the meaning of true love. The Christian concept of love embodies a willingness to serve others without consideration for what they can do for you (Matthew 6:3,4). Its motivation springs from a sense of love and obedience for our Lord (Colossians 3:23-24). We love because God loves us. Our love is patterned after the life of Christ, "Here is my servant whom I have chosen, the one I love, in whom I delight; I will put my Spirit on him, and he will proclaim justice to the nations. He will not quarrel or cry out; no one will hear his voice in the streets. A bruised reed he will not break, and a smoldering wick he will not snuff out, till he leads justice to victory. In his name the nations will put their hope" (Matthew 12:18-21).

However, being the servant of Christ does not mean servitude to manipulation. When material aid is given impersonally, some people become shrewd players of the game. An individual must listen closely to the Holy Spirit in ministry and grow in a sense of discernment. One urban church food pantry discontinued their gift of free food to a particular alcoholic once they learned he would sell their gift of food to buy a drink. Servanthood may mean tough love.

True Christian servanthood is focused upon enabling others rather than building one's own image or "religious kingdom." Jesus quickly confronted this temptation in his early disciples, "You know that the rulers of the Gentiles lord it over them, and their high officials exercise authority over them. Not so with you. Instead, whoever wants to become great among you must be your servant, and whoever wants to be first must be your slave — just as the Son of Man did not come to be served, but to serve, and to give his life as a ransom for many" (Matthew 20:25-28). Success is seen not in the power that can be accumulated, but the empowerment given to others.

4. Enhancement of Christian Community. Care giving has been compartmentalized and isolated in many urban centers. Intricate independent structures exist for education, judicial, political, health, social, and religious institutions. Lack of community intercommunication has led to the disintegration of cooperation. This is true even of many urban churches whose members drive long distances once a week to worship. Members absent from the immediate community make the church's community witness difficult.

Other churches may seek to retreat psychologically from the problems of the urban community or "the world." Rather than helping their members receive guidance and encouragement to live in the principles of the Kingdom of God in their daily existence, the focus becomes heaven. A critical comment I have heard in Cabrini is, "The church has become so heavenly minded it is no earthly good."

The message of hope, authentic messengers and a ministry of servanthood should result in a strong Christian community. The Christian life is not merely a mystical experience between an individual and God. The dual commandments of Christ portray the central focus of how one's faith should result in love for those around them. Jesus said, "'Love the Lord your God with all your heart and with all your soul and with all your mind.' This is the first and greatest commandment. And the second is like it: 'Love your neighbor as yourself.' All the Law and Prophets stand on these two commandments" (Matthew 22:37-40).

This central aspect of the Christian life was also underscored by the disciple John, "We love because he first loved us. If anyone says, 'I love God,' yet hates his brother, he is a liar. For anyone who does not love his brother, whom he has seen, cannot love God, whom he has not seen. And he has given us this command: Whoever loves God must love his brother" (1 John 4:19-21).

The urban church can stand as a refuge for individuals, marriages and families who are seeking a caring community in a society which treats them as anonymous entities. In urban areas where people are often transient, it is important that the church offer a place of stability. Individuals need to know that the church will be present in the midst of their pain. Yet, earning the right to be heard often takes time; trust has to be nurtured. If care givers are here today and gone tomorrow, deep relationships and trust cannot take root in the lives of people.

The church can become a center for the community where people are not only drawn towards God, but closer to each other and equipped to provide God's witness in their community. A sense of support from a community of believers can encourage members to develop their individual spiritual gifts (1 Corinthians 12:12-31). Scriptural principles can become guidelines for genuine love of others (1 Corinthians 13). Through an atmosphere of love, individuals can be nurtured and challenged to grow.

The knowledge of the systemic problems in Cabrini-Green and the injustice people suffer are the hardest part of ministry here. My frustration comes in not knowing how to address the systems which cause their pain. In the city which witnessed the settlement houses of Jane Addams, a Quaker, and later Saul Alinsky's community organizing, we are still struggling for answers.

I rejoice as individuals respond to the Lord's will for their lives. Hope grows as we unite to live the message of Christ in our community. My prayer echoes the words of the prophet Isaiah which were embraced by Christ Jesus early in his ministry:

> The Spirit of the Sovereign Lord is on me,
> because the Lord has anointed me
> to preach good news to the poor.
> He has sent me to bind up the brokenhearted,
> to proclaim freedom for the captives,
> and release for the prisoners,
> to proclaim the year of the Lord's favor
> and the day of vengeance of our God,
> to comfort all who mourn,

and provide for those who grieve in Zion —
to bestow on them a crown of beauty instead of ashes,
the oil of gladness instead of mourning,
and a garment of praise instead of despair.
They will be called oaks of righteousness,
a planting of the Lord for the display of his splendor.
They will rebuild the ancient ruins
and restore the places long devastated;
they will renew the ruined cities that have been devastated
for generations.

Isaiah 61:1-4

DATE DUE

HIGHSMITH   # 45220